"This is one of the best comprehensive books I have read in my long hypnotherapy career."
—*Daniel L. Araoz*

"Dr. Yapko has been practicing hypnosis for a number of years and brings that rich experience to bear in this book. Designed as an information-packed introduction for those with little knowledge of hypnosis and the use of hypnosis in clinical practice, *Essentials of Hypnosis* can be recommended not only for the beginner but for the more experienced reader. Its coverage is thorough, and there is a very rich citation of books and articles covering principles and practice."
—ERNEST R. HILGARD, PH.D.,
Professor of Psychology Emeritus,
Stanford University

"A clear guide for the perplexed! A fine text for the beginner seeking a balanced view of The New Hypnosis." —ERNEST L. ROSSI, PH.D.,
Private Practice, Malibu, California

"Dr. Yapko has written a concise and comprehensive introduction to the field of hypnosis. It is easy to read and replete with current references. I warmly recommend it to anyone seeking an overview of the subject written from the perspective of a leader in the field."
—ALEXANDER A. LEVITAN, M.D., M.P.H.,
Past President, American Society of Clinical Hypnosis;
Past President, American Board of Medical Hypnosis

"With the clarity for which he is well known, Dr. Yapko gives us a unique reference source of current hypnosis. This is one of the best comprehensive books I have read in my long hypnotherapy career. It has clarified for me important aspects of the new hypnosis of Milton Erickson. *Essentials of Hypnosis* will soon become a key volume for serious students of clinical hypnosis."
—DANIEL L. ARAOZ, ED.D., ABPP, ABPH,
Executive Director,
Long Island Institute of Ericksonian Hypnosis

"Michael Yapko is an exemplary teacher who knows his stuff about hypnosis. He is clear and comprehensive."
—WILLIAM O'HANLON, M.S.,
Author, Solution-Oriented Hypnosis

"Dr. Michael Yapko has succeeded in writing a valuable reference book. It is clear, concise, informative, interesting, and readable, and it contains a very extensive bibliography. It's a solid and comprehensive, yet succinct, review of the entire field of hypnosis."

—BRIAN M. ALMAN, PH.D.,
Author, Self-Hypnosis

"Learning the fundamentals of modern clinical hypnosis is as simple as reading this book. Michael Yapko has a gifted ability to comprehensively present building blocks that will edify the novice and serve as important reminders for the experienced practitioner. An essential primer of essential concepts." —JEFFREY K. ZEIG, PH.D.,
Director of the Milton H. Erickson Foundation

"This is a wonderful primer that will help to clarify what can be expected from hypnosis. I will be using it in my office to demystify and educate clients and beginning trainees who seek a strong intellectual foundation to clinical hypnosis."

—STEPHEN LANKTON, M.S.W., D.A.H.B.,
Diplomate in Clinical Hypnosis,
American Hypnosis Board for Clinical Social Work;
Approved Consultant in Clinical Hypnosis,
American Society for Clinical Hypnosis

About the Brunner/Mazel Basic Principles Into Practice Series

These volumes provide essential fundamentals of theory and technique and are intended as primers for interested laypeople, as basic texts for both graduate and undergraduate courses, and as introductions for practicing psychotherapists. *Essentials of Hypnosis* is Volume 4 of this important new series. Previously published titles are as follows:

1. Family Therapy: Fundamentals of Theory and Practice
   By William A. Griffin, Ph.D.
2. Essentials of Psychoanalysis
   By Herbert S. Strean, D.S.W.
3. Understanding Mental Disorders Due to Medical Conditions or Substance Abuse: What Every Therapist Should Know
   By Ghazi Asaad, M.D.

Upcoming titles will cover topics such as Attention Deficit Hyperactivity Disorder; Child Abuse; Psychosomatic Disorders; Using Metaphors in Therapy; Working with Stepfamilies; Ericksonian Psychotherapy; Child Therapy; Drama Therapy; Clinical Social Work; and others.

BRUNNER/MAZEL
BASIC PRINCIPLES INTO PRACTICE SERIES
VOLUME 4

ESSENTIALS
OF
HYPNOSIS

MICHAEL D. YAPKO, Ph.D.

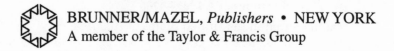
BRUNNER/MAZEL, *Publishers* • NEW YORK
A member of the Taylor & Francis Group

Library of Congress Cataloging-in-Publication Data

Yapko, Michael D.
    Essentials of hypnosis / Michael D. Yapko
        p. cm.— (Brunner/Mazel basic principles into
practice series; v. 4)
  Includes bibliographical references and index.
  ISBN 0-87630-761-6
  1. Hypnotism—Therapeutic use. I. Title. II. Series:
Brunner/Mazel basic principles into practice library; v.4.
RC495.Y368 1995
616.89'162—dc20

                                      94-30541
                                          CIP

Published by
Brunner/Mazel
A member of the Taylor & Francis Group
47 Runway road, Suite G
Levittown, PA 19057-4700

Manufactured in the United States of America
10 9 8 7 6 5 4

In loving memory of my grandmother, Mollie Cooper, Gal Friday to all of us in more ways than one. And in loving memory of my grandparents, Betty and Sol Kemp, who understood the wonders of ice cream and princesses. They each gave me a lot to look back on...

and

With love to Megan Leigh Horowitz, "The Hugbug," who gives me a lot to look forward to.

Contents

Preface

When Natalie Gilman, the talented senior editor at Brunner/Mazel Publishers, called to tell me about a new book series they intended to publish called "Basic Principles Into Practice," she described it as creating a series of introductory level books on various topics in the field of psychotherapy. These would serve not only as basic guides for the novice, but also as refresher courses for practicing professionals. What a great idea! With so much information available in any particular area one might choose to learn about, an overview approach seems a wonderful way to give people who are new to the topic a good sense of what's going on in that area without completely overwhelming them. And, if and when their appetite to learn more is whetted, there could be plenty of current references included to point them in the right direction.

So, that's how this book came about. It is short but information-packed. It provides perspective on the field of clinical hypnosis. It raises many clinical issues and encourages you to think critically about them. It suggests methods and applications. It lets you know at all times that there is a great deal of research and practical written material to be found in the broad body of literature of the field of hypnosis. And, it tells you where a lot of that material can be found when you want to know more. In fact, the reference sections at the end of each chapter are a primary feature of this book since all of the chapters are purposely general and brief in order to simply acquaint you with the topic at hand.

Much of this book is derived from my comprehensive textbook, *Trancework*. Much has been trimmed while some new sections have been added, all with "succinct" as the defining adjective. This is a bare-to-the-bones text, in line with the larger goal of the *Brunner/Mazel Basic Principles Into Practice Series*.

Hypnosis is an inherently fascinating topic. Whatever you have already seen and heard about it has probably piqued your curiosity enough to lead you to this book. When you get past the silly magical connotations hypnosis seems to conjure up in most people, and you learn about it instead as a serious tool widely applicable in clinical contexts, I think it gets even more interesting. How you can say and do things purposefully that can generate amazing responses in people, like vivid memories they can relive or a perception of detachment from their bodies sufficient to have surgery with no chemical anesthesia, *is* truly amazing. The field of hypnosis is dynamic, diverse, and ever-growing. I hope the serious possibilities—as well as the wonder of it all—come through to you in these pages.

Michael D. Yapko, Ph.D.
Solana Beach, California

Acknowledgments

Brunner/Mazel has been my professional publishing home for many years, this being the fifth book I have done with them. Mark Tracten, the owner of Brunner/Mazel, is not just my publisher, he's also my friend. I appreciate his support and willingness to help my work see the light of day. Natalie Gilman, my editor, is superb to work with. I thank her for including me in the *Basic Principles Into Practice Series*.

I have many professional friends and colleagues who deserve special mention for their valuable contributions to me. Each of the people mentioned below is special to me, each in his or her own way. Lively debate, enlightened discussion, professional respect, and friendship all mark my relationship with these wonderful people who have been so influential in my work:

Brian Alman	John Koriath
Norma and Phil Barretta	Doris Murphy
MaryBeth Chruden	Marian Richetta
Stephen Gilligan	Jeff Zeig

My closest work partner is Linda Griebel, a woman of integrity who does a fantastic job of keeping things running smoothly. Many years and many projects later, my appreciation for Linda keeps growing.

On the personal side, I want to acknowledge my family and friends. The Yapko and Harris families are wonderfully loving and supportive. Wendy and Richard Horowitz, to whom that incredible Megan Leigh (the captor of my heart) belongs, are the best friends imaginable. With a touch of humor yet with sincerity, I want to acknowledge: 1) The Ghirardelli Chocolate Factory in San Francisco. If they gave Nobel Prizes for chocolate, these folks would win hands-down; 2) Captain Jean-Luc Picard, of the Starship Enterprise, who is the metaphorical embodiment of clarity and integrity; 3) Starbucks Coffee, for incomparable cafe mochas; 4) Jethro Tull and Eric Clapton, for exquisite auditory pleasures; and, finally, 5) whoever invented ice cream.

Last, but most important of all, is my wife, Diane. Simply the best. Really. *The very best.*

M.D.Y.

ESSENTIALS
OF
HYPNOSIS

Section I

PRINCIPLES

1

PERSPECTIVES

This book is not intended to sensationalize hypnosis, nor is it intended to make a statement about how hypnosis is the answer to all of life's challenges. Rather, I will introduce clinical hypnosis as a system of skilled and influential communication that teaches how *words can heal.* Clinical hypnosis offers ways to conceptualize how human beings construct their individual realities, and it offers insights into ways to interact more effectively with others. Acquiring hypnotic skills is one way to enhance your clinical abilities, and can help you to obtain lasting results in the therapy work you do. Perhaps best of all, the use of hypnosis can be a powerful way to promote self-sufficiency and independence in the clients you treat, helping them to be more self-assured and self-valuing.

Clinical hypnosis is a skill of using words and gestures in particular ways to achieve specific outcomes. The emphasis throughout this volume will be on the use of hypnotic processes as agents of *effective communication* and *change.* This orientation minimizes the use of incantations and rituals in its use, instead emphasizing a rapid assessment of and sensitive responsiveness to individual client needs.

Few fields have had the ups and downs hypnosis has had. Hypnosis has been around, in various forms, for thousands of years. Acceptability has varied from moderate to none. People who practiced hypnosis had their rituals (techniques) and superstitions ("This induction worked pretty well on the last client I had with freckles..."), but very little cognitive understanding of what they were doing. With the acceptability and applicability of hypnotic processes growing in scope, the need for a sensible, understandable approach seems greater than ever before.

When people discover I use hypnosis as a tool in my clinical practice, typically they are both fascinated and skeptical. Almost everyone has had some direct or indirect experience with hypnosis, and it is incorrectly assumed that whatever I do with it must basically be the same as

3

whatever anyone and everyone else who uses hypnosis does with it. Few people have had enough exposure to hypnosis to be able to differentiate the different types and applications of hypnosis from one another. Clinical hypnosis is not the same as research hypnosis, or sports hypnosis, or entertainment hypnosis. Even the clinicians using hypnosis will each use it very differently from one another. This is a slight drawback to being a practitioner of therapeutic hypnosis; the general public too often assumes that "hypnosis is hypnosis is hypnosis," and that all they have to do as consumers is shop around to find the most inexpensive deal with the most promises attached. And some of the promises are nothing short of outrageous!

Used skillfully, however, this problem can become an asset. By exploring with the consumer seeking information about hypnosis in general or about my work in particular, I can help the person become knowledgeable enough to make some meaningful decisions. Making certain that clients have the information necessary to make an informed decision about treatment should, in my opinion, be basic to any professional practice. Just because someone doesn't ask questions does not mean he or she has none. It usually means the person just doesn't know what to ask.

By involving people in a brief discussion about their needs and the nature of clinical hypnosis as a tool, you can provide information that helps clients more realistically assess their needs, and the best means for meeting them. Often, formal hypnosis aimed at symptom removal alone (like that of newspaper ads that scream, "Stop smoking in one session!") is not a desirable or realistic treatment alternative. However, it is often sought after by individuals seeking "magic" and a chance to avoid the maze of more personally demanding or threatening approaches to treatment. Sometimes, such superficial approaches work exactly the way they say they will. Why? Read on...

The fact that hypnosis is used as a stage act in the media (live shows especially, but also in cinema and television) contributes to popular stereotypes portraying hypnosis as a magical means for instant problem-resolution through powerful suggestions. I wish I had a nickel for every person who has asked for a "quick suggestion" to stop some bad habit. Rational explanations about why the work to be done might be a little more involved than they think are often met with puzzled looks and some variation of the question, "Then how does a stage hypnotist just snap his fingers to get his subject to do whatever he wants him to?" People often think you can finger-snap away complex problems. Unrealistic concepts can lead to disappointment and disillusionment in such clients.

Explaining the purposes and capabilities of hypnosis as a therapeutic tool is almost always beneficial for people. Clarification of expectations usually leads the client to face the fact that there are no miracle cures to be promised. It means accepting personal responsibility for one's problems, and it means being active in their resolution.

Just as dangerous as the stage hypnotist in promoting misconceptions is the hypnotist who, through ignorance or greed, uses hypnosis in a practice that caters to public misconception. Such persons usually have little or no formal education in hypnosis and the healing sciences, but know just enough to mislead people with false claims of sensational power.

These are just a few insights into the problems faced by clinical hypnosis as a field. Others are discussed in later sections of this book. The point is made throughout that if hypnosis is to be considered a serious treatment alternative, it must be promoted with a sensitivity to the issues that concern both clients and other health-care providers. Your interest in learning about hypnosis is a wonderful beginning. My goal is to guide that interest in the direction of developing an appreciation for the many innovative and extraordinary ways hypnosis can be used sensibly in clinical practice to help those in need.

SUGGESTED READINGS

The following suggested readings are general texts that provide good diverse overviews of the field of hypnosis.

Araoz, D. (1985). *The new hypnosis.* New York: Brunner/Mazel.

Barber, T. (1969). *Hypnosis: A scientific approach.* New York: Van Nostrand Reinhold.

Brown, D. & Fromm, E. (1986). *Hypnotherapy and hypnoanalysis.* Hillsdale, NJ: Erlbaum.

Cheek, D. & LeCron, L. (1968). *Clinical hypnotherapy.* New York: Grune & Stratton.

Clark, J. & Jackson, J. (1983). *Hypnosis and behavior therapy.* New York: Springer.

Fromm, E. & Nash, M. (Eds.) (1992). *Contemporary hypnosis research.* New York: Guilford.

Gilligan, S. (1987). *Therapeutic trances: The cooperation principle in Ericksonian hypnotherapy.* New York: Brunner/Mazel.

Hammond, D. (Ed.) (1990). *Handbook of hypnotic suggestions and metaphors.* New York: Norton.

Hilgard, E. (1965). *Hypnotic susceptibility.* New York: Harcourt, Brace and World.

King, M. & Citrenbaum, C. (1993). *Existential hypnotherapy.* New York: Guilford.

Kroger, W. (1977). *Clinical and experimental hypnosis in medicine, dentistry and psychology* (2nd ed.). Philadelphia: Lippincott.

O'Hanlon, W. (1987). *Taproots: Underlying principles of Milton Erickson's therapy and hypnosis.* New York: Norton.

O'Hanlon, W. & Martin, M. (1992). *Solution-oriented hypnosis.* New York: Norton.

Sarbin, T. & Coe, W. (1972). *Hypnosis: A social psychological analysis of influence communication.* New York: Holt, Rinehart and Winston.

Spiegel, H. & Spiegel, D. (1987). *Trance and treatment: Clinical uses of hypnosis.* Washington, DC: American Psychiatric Press.

Weitzenhoffer, A. (1989). *The practice of hypnotism* (Vols. 1&2). New York: John Wiley & Sons.

Wright, M. & Wright, S. (1987). *Clinical practice of hypnotherapy.* New York: Guilford.

Yapko, M. (1990). *Trancework: An introduction to the practice of clinical hypnosis* (2nd ed.). New York: Brunner/Mazel.

Zeig, J. (Ed.) (1982). *Ericksonian approaches to hypnosis and psychotherapy.* New York: Brunner/Mazel.

2

BROADENING PERSPECTIVES

Hypnosis as a word has been overused to the point of its being robbed of any real meaning. When one word comes to describe as many different experiences as "hypnosis" has, there is ample opportunity for misunderstanding, mislabeling, misconception, and, ultimately, confusion. To date, there is no commonly accepted definition of hypnosis, nor does one seem forthcoming. Likewise, as you will see later, there is no single unifying theory to account for all the various facets of hypnosis. Some prominent theorists, researchers, and practitioners have noted this with frustration and asked that more attention be paid to the need for greater clarity as to the nature of hypnosis (Hall, 1989; Hilgard, 1973, 1991; Lynn & Rhue, 1991; Rossi, 1993).

It is precisely because hypnosis is one word for so many different experiences that the average person comes to believe that "hypnosis is hypnosis," regardless of the context in which it is applied. Even well educated professionals who are untrained in hypnosis are often skeptical about its use in clinical contexts. They wonder whether it differs appreciably from the silly things they've seen demonstrated in stage shows.

Advocates of hypnosis have long recognized this tendency, generally feeling more misunderstood as a group than others. Yet, the term remains virtually unchanged in common usage.

Arranging the concepts and techniques of hypnosis into a useful definition is a difficult task, to say the least. Moving in that direction, though, others' perspectives may be useful for the purpose of illustrating the wide range of views of hypnosis in the field. If you were to review various definitions of hypnosis, you would typically find offerings such as these:

1. Hypnosis is guided imagination. The hypnotist, either another person (heterohypnosis) or one's self (autohypnosis, self-hypnosis) acts as a guide for an experience regarded as fantasy (Barber, 1979; Barber, Spanos & Chaves, 1974).
2. Hypnosis is a natural, altered state of consciousness. The person enters a hypnotic state, a state distinctly different from the person's "normal" state, through a natural process not involving ingestion of any substances or other physical treatments (Ludwig, 1966; Ludwig & Levine, 1965; Tart, 1969).
3. Hypnosis is a relaxed, hypersuggestible state. The person enters a very relaxed state of mind and body, and subsequently is more responsive to suggestion (Edmonston, 1991; Miller, 1979).
4. Hypnosis is a state of intense concentration, focusing and maximizing involvement with one idea or sensory stimulus at a time (Spiegel & Spiegel, 1987).

The process of clinical intervention can be described as a series of communications exchanged between the clinician and client (Araoz, 1985; Watzlawick, 1978). No matter what your therapeutic orientation, you are using the communications of your client to make assessments about him or her, and you are using your communications as the vehicle for your therapy. A therapeutic communication is one that somehow influences the person in distress to feel or behave differently in a way that is considered adaptive or beneficial (Zeig & Rennick, 1991).

The essence of what I am discussing here is communication and interpersonal influence, and that is precisely where hypnosis comes in. If you reject the passive view of hypnosis as simply some individual's subjective internal state, and instead you consider the dynamics of interpersonal communication that a clinician employs in order to influence a client to have a suggested therapeutic experience, then a rich and complex new world opens up. Somewhere in the communications of both the hypnotist and the psychotherapist are specific components that enable a client's subjective experience to be altered and therapeutic influence to take place (Watzlawick, 1985). Approaching hypnosis from this interactional standpoint places emphasis on being an effective communicator. That means you are able to recognize others' styles of thought and then competently organize your communications in ways that maximize their chances for being understood at one or more levels, then integrated in ways that prove beneficial (Gilligan, 1987).

When you shift your way of thinking about hypnosis (and therapy, too, for that matter) to focus on dimensions of communication that increase the potential for influencing another person's experience, the emphasis is much less on ritual and attaining particular levels of hypnosis, and much more on the use of words and gestures in specific ways (Haley, 1973). Thus, elements of *any* piece of communication can have hypnotic (i.e., absorbing and influential) qualities without formally being "hypnosis" (Watzlawick, 1985). This point in particular allows the study of hypnosis to be of even greater potential value for anyone who works with people. Even if you choose not to pursue expertise in doing formal hypnosis, you can still benefit greatly from learning about the various aspects of effective communication. After all, one insensitively used word or phrase can hinder or even prevent a positive treatment result. Likewise, a sensitively used word or phrase can foster a positive belief that dramatically improves the chances for a successful result.

I think it important to recognize the ever present nature of interpersonal influence. In one course I have taught many times, Social Psychology, I usually make the statement at the start of class that "you will do things when you are by yourself that you will not do as soon as even just one other person is around."* Recognizing hypnotic elements in everyday situations is a skill that can allow you to use hypnosis more flexibly and with greater success (Erickson, 1958).

By defining clinical hypnosis as a process of influential communication, I am de-emphasizing the need to perform structured hypnotic rituals in order to obtain hypnosis, which is what I call "formal hypnosis." The growing popularity of indirect techniques of hypnosis to complement more direct methods is the direct result of the recognition that a person's experience can be guided and hypnotic responses are possible without any formal induction taking place at all (Wagstaff, 1991; Watzlawick, 1985). Since hypnosis is, in some ways, an everyday experience, all a good hypnotist does is create hypnotic phenomena deliberately instead of waiting for them to occur randomly. No hypnotist is creating experiences outside the realm of what occurs routinely in people in other contexts. When I describe the hypnotic phenomena to you later, this point will become much clearer.

Defining hypnosis as a process of influential communication is an extremely, almost embarrassingly, general definition. As so often hap-

---

* The point, of course, is that the mere presence of another person alters your behavior. It is not a question of *whether* you will influence people — you undoubtedly will — but rather a question of *how* you will influence them. Learning to use patterns of influence responsibly while respecting the integrity of those we work with is a demanding challenge. Patterns of influence do not just exist in the contexts of therapy or hypnosis, though. If you are observant, you will see them literally everywhere that you see social interaction.

pens when one tries to define abstract concepts, a more precise definition can be provided only when the variables of a specific context can
be considered. I am suggesting flexible, situational definitions of hypnosis. Included in such definitions would be the client's subjective
experience, noticeably absent from the discussion thus far and discussed at length later.

REFERENCES

Araoz, D. (1985). *The new hypnosis.* New York: Brunner/Mazel.

Barber, J. (1972). Suggested "hypnotic" behavior: The trance paradigm vs. an
   alternative paradigm. In E. Fromm & R. Shor (Eds.), *Hypnosis: Research
   developments and perspectives.* Chicago, IL: Aldine Atherton.

Barber, T., Spanos, N. & Chaves, J. (1974). *Hypnotism: Imagination and human
   potentialities.* Elmsford, NY: Pergamon.

Edmonston, W. (1991). Anesis. In S. Lynn & J. Rhue (Eds.), *Theories of hypnosis:
   Current models and perspectives* (pp. 197–237). New York: Guilford.

Erickson, M. (1958). Naturalistic techniques of hypnosis. *American Journal of
   Clinical Hypnosis, 1,* 3–8.

Gilligan, S. (1987). *Therapeutic trances: The cooperation principle in Ericksonian
   hypnotherapy.* New York: Brunner/Mazel.

Haley, J. (1973). *Uncommon therapy: The psychiatric techniques of Milton H.
   Erickson, M.D.* New York: Norton.

Hall, J. (1989). *Hypnosis: A Jungian perspective.* New York: Guilford.

Hilgard, E. (1973). The domain of hypnosis, with some comments on alternative
   paradigms. *American Psychologist, 28,* 972–982.

Hilgard, E. (1991). A neodissociation interpretation of hypnosis. In S. Lynn & J.
   Rhue (Eds.), *Theories of hypnosis: Current models and perspectives* (pp. 83–
   104). New York: Guilford.

Ludwig, A. (1966). Altered states of consciousness. *Archives of General Psychiatry,
   15,* 225–234.

Ludwig, A. & Levine, J. (1965). Alterations in consciousness produced by hypnosis.
   Journal of Nervous and Mental Diseases, 140, 146–153.

Lynn, S. & Rhue, J. (1991). An integrative model of hypnosis. In S. Lynn & J. Rhue
   (Eds.), *Theories of hypnosis: Current models and perspectives* (pp. 397–438).
   New York: Guilford.

Miller, M. (1979). *Therapeutic hypnosis.* New York: Human Sciences Press.

Rossi, E. (1993). *The psychobiology of mind-body healing* (Rev. ed.). New York:
   Norton.

Spiegel, H. & Spiegel, D. (1987). *Trance and treatment: Clinical uses of hypnosis.*
   Washington, DC: American Psychiatric Press.

Tart, C. (Ed.) (1969). *Altered states of consciousness: A book of readings.* New York:
   John Wiley & Sons.

Wagstaff, G. (1991). Compliance, belief, and semantics in hypnosis: A nonstate,
   sociocognitive perspective. In S. Lynn & J. Rhue (Eds.), *Theories of hypnosis:*

Current models and perspectives (pp. 362–396). New York: Guilford.

Watzlawick, P. (1978). *The language of change.* New York: Basic Books.

Watzlawick, P. (1985). Hypnotherapy without trance. In J. Zeig (Ed.), *Ericksonian psychotherapy, Vol. 1: Structures* (pp. 5–14). New York: Brunner/Mazel.

Zeig, J. & Rennick, P. (1991). Ericksonian hypnotherapy: A communications approach to hypnosis. In S. Lynn & J. Rhue (Eds.), *Theories of hypnosis: Current models and perspectives* (pp. 275–302). New York: Guilford.

3

THE ORIGINS OF MYTH

In the practice of clinical hypnosis, the opportunity for dealing with misinformation is constant. Most misconceptions are predictable, which can make their identification and correction easier. Most people hold the stereotypical view of hypnosis as a powerful form of mind control, and the most common misconceptions are based on that notion (Levitan & Jevne, 1986; Mann, 1986; Udolf, 1981; Wester, 1984).

Involving the client in a discussion about his or her beliefs and expectations for the hypnotic and psychotherapeutic experiences is necessary to make certain he or she is knowledgeable enough to make sensible decisions about treatment. Since the client's understanding of the process is likely to be inaccurate, incomplete, or both, the ethical and competent professional can provide the person with as much information as he or she may require in order to participate in the process in a cooperative and positive way. You'll note I say as much information should be provided as the person "requires," implying that on some occasions the amount of information dispensed may be marginal, while in other instances it is substantial. Individual needs differ, and only by communicating clearly with your client will you discover what his or her needs are. Generally, though, a well-informed client is in a much better position to make the therapy a more meaningful collaboration (Kirsch & Council, 1992).

Only by engaging the person seeking help in a discussion about his or her beliefs and expectations can you discover how much he or she knows and how much he or she knows that isn't so. Three basic questions that have been useful for me to ask are: Have you ever had experience with hypnosis before? Was it personal experience or was it something you saw, read, or heard about? What impressions did you form?

If the client has had personal experience with hypnosis, good questions to ask might include: What was the situation in which you experienced hypnosis? Who was the hypnotist and what were his or her qualifications? What was the explanation given to you about hypnosis at the time? What techniques were used with you? Was it a successful experience? Why or why not? How did you feel about the experience? What is the basis for your seeking further experience with hypnosis? The information you gather will be vital in determining your approach. Asking a lot of questions can sometimes be threatening and tiresome to the client, and so must be done gently; interrogations under a bright light are not recommended (Erickson & Rossi, 1979; Moore, 1982).

If the person has not had any personal experience with hypnosis, then good questions to ask might include: Have you ever seen hypnosis demonstrated? Have you heard about hypnosis before? In what context? How have you heard hypnosis may be used? Do you know anyone personally who has experienced hypnosis? If so, how did he or she describe the experience? In asking some or all of these questions, you learn about the client's experiences and attitudes concerning hypnosis. Then misconceptions can be dealt with, unrealistic fears can be alleviated, and a positive belief system can be encouraged (Weitzenhoffer, 1957; Zilbergeld, 1986).

It is especially important to ask about specific hypnotic techniques the client may have previously experienced. If he or she experienced a procedure that was either ineffective or unpleasant, then using a similar technique is one way of assuring a similar failure. Unless you specifically ask about prior experience, you run the risk of unwittingly duplicating past negative experiences.

If the client has not had personal experience with hypnosis before, but is only indirectly familiar with it through the entertainment media or the experiences of an acquaintance, it becomes even more important to discover his or her beliefs and attitudes. Second- and third-hand stories from "knowledgeable" friends often have a tendency to get distorted, and they can sometimes be as misleading as the entertainer's version of hypnosis. Many clients are fearful of the "mind-control" potential, but seek the associated "magic wand" for quick results (Thompson, 1988).

The major issue that arises for most people, experienced with hypnosis or not, is that of "control." The client's fear of losing control is the single greatest obstacle you are likely to encounter. In one form or another, almost every common misconception is related to this fear. Unless you acknowledge and deal with it in a sensitive and positive way, it will undoubtedly hinder or even prevent the attainment of therapeutic results. The belief that hypnosis has the power to take self-control away from an individual has been fostered in all the ways mentioned previously. Until one has had the experience of therapeutic hypnosis in a positive atmosphere of caring and professionalism, the fear can seem realistic (Murray-Jobsis, 1986).

REFERENCES

Erickson, M. & Rossi, E. (1979). *Hypnotherapy: An exploratory casebook.* New York: Irvington.

Kirsch, I. & Council, J. (1992). Situational and personality correlates of hypnotic responsiveness. In E. Fromm & M. Nash (Eds.), *Contemporary hypnosis research* (pp. 267–291). New York: Guilford.

Levitan, A. & Jevne, R. (1986). Patients fearful of hypnosis. In B. Zilbergeld, M. Edelstein & D. Araoz (Eds.), *Hypnosis: Questions and answers* (pp. 81–86). New York: Norton.

Mann, H. (1986). Describing hypnosis to patients. In B. Zilbergeld, M. Edelstein & D. Araoz (Eds.), *Hypnosis: Questions and answers* (pp. 76–80). New York: Norton.

Moore, M. (1982). Principles of Ericksonian induction of hypnosis. In J. Zeig (Ed.), *Ericksonian approaches to hypnosis and psychotherapy* (pp. 101–112). New York: Brunner/Mazel.

Murray-Jobsis, J. (1986). Patients who claim they are not hypnotizable. In B. Zilbergeld, M. Edelstein & D. Araoz (Eds.), *Hypnosis: Questions and answers* (pp. 91–94). New York: Norton.

Thompson, K. (1988). Motivation and the multiple states of trance. In J. Zeig & S. Lankton (Eds.), *Developing Ericksonian therapy: State of the art* (pp. 149–163). New York: Brunner/Mazel.

Udolf, R. (1981). *Handbook of hypnosis for professionals.* New York: Van Nostrand Reinhold.

Weitzenhoffer, A. (1957). *General techniques of hypnotism.* New York: Grune & Stratton.

Wester, W. (1984). Preparing the patient. In W. Wester & A. Smith (Eds.), *Clinical hypnosis: A multi-disciplinary approach* (pp. 18–28). Philadelphia: Lippincott.

Zilbergeld, B. (1986). Choosing inductions. In B. Zilbergeld, M. Edelstein & D. Araoz (Eds.), *Hypnosis: Questions and answers* (pp. 103–109). New York: Norton.

4

RESPONDING TO MISCONCEPTIONS

Taking the time to identify and correct misconceptions can help you sidestep the issue of control, particularly if you emphasize the naturalistic nature of hypnosis through your use of everyday examples of hypnosis taken directly from the client's routine experience (Erickson & Rossi, 1979; Golden, 1986). Furthermore, you can reinforce for the client the virtually total self-control the hypnotized person maintains during the hypnotic experience. Clinicians have to be sensitive to the issue of control and respond to it in some meaningful way, either directly or indirectly. Avoiding the issue of control can be anxiety-producing for the already uncertain client and may create a force ("resistance") that works against the aims of treatment. If a client senses an imminent loss of control, the typical result is a power struggle with the clinician. Would *you* want to be hypnotized if you thought you would lose control of yourself? The goal is to do all you can to avoid a power struggle and to define the relationship as a cooperative one (Gilligan, 1982; Grinder & Bandler, 1981). After all, there really is no way to win a power struggle with the client; to win, all he or she has to do is *nothing!*

There is a paradox present in hypnosis and psychotherapy. Jay Haley (1963) described this paradox in terms of the hypnotist's seemingly contradictory message: "I can only hypnotize you by you hypnotizing yourself: I can only help you by you helping yourself." Essentially, the message emphasizes the responsibility and control on the part of the client, which are then shared with the clinician. If I say to you, "Here. I am giving you control of me," then who is really in control? If I have the control, then all I am really doing is suspending my decision to exercise my choices and instead using yours. I remain free, though, to begin exercising my choices again at any time I either have to or want to.

Identifying and correcting misconceptions alleviates fear and uncertainty, and encourages realistic expectations. Unrealistic expectations at either extreme of wanting hypnosis to be a "magic wand" that can effect instantaneous cures for complex problems or, conversely, feeling the problem is hopeless altogether are expectations that are likely to reduce therapy's effectiveness. Such obstacles are unnecessary; you can avoid them by providing correct information and securing an informed consent to treatment (Kroger, 1977; Spiegel & Spiegel, 1987).

Described in the remainder of this chapter are the most frequently encountered misconceptions about clinical hypnosis. As you become more familiar with hypnosis, responding to these and other misconceptions will likely become automatic. You may be surprised how many people, including "hypnotists," believe some of these erroneous ideas.

MISCONCEPTION: HYPNOSIS IS CAUSED BY THE POWER OF THE HYPNOTIST

In the clinical context, the hypnotist is able to use his or her skills in communication to make acceptance of suggestions by the client more likely, but there is no control over the client other than whatever degree of control the client gives to the hypnotist. If you allow someone to guide you through a suggested experience, who is in control? The hypnotist may direct the client's experience, but only to the degree that the client permits it. It is clearly a relationship of mutual responsiveness (Gilligan, 1987; Stanton, 1985).

MISCONCEPTION: ONLY CERTAIN KINDS OF PEOPLE CAN BE HYPNOTIZED

In practice, there are definitely some people more difficult to induce hypnosis in than others. Such persons are not usually less capable than others, but they are less responsive for any of a wide range of reasons, such as: they fear losing control, they have a hard time distinguishing ambiguous (for them) internal states such as tension or relaxation, they fear impending changes, they're aware of negative situational factors, and so forth. When the nature of the resistance is identified and resolved, the "difficult" person can often be transformed from a poor hypnotic subject into a reasonably good one (Araoz, 1985; Barber, 1980).

MISCONCEPTION: ANYONE WHO CAN BE HYPNOTIZED MUST BE WEAK-MINDED

Since virtually all people enter spontaneous, informal hypnotic states regularly, the ability to be hypnotized is not reliably correlated with specific personality traits. This particular misconception refers to the Svengali image of the all-powerful hypnotist, and is based on the belief that in order for a hypnotist to control someone, the individual must have little or no will of his or her own (Weitzenhoffer, 1989).

MISCONCEPTION: ONCE ONE HAS BEEN HYPNOTIZED, ONE CAN NO LONGER RESIST IT

This misconception refers to the idea that a hypnotist controls the will of his or her subject, and that once you "succumb to the power" of the hypnotist, you are forever at his or her mercy. Of course, nothing is farther from the truth, since the hypnotic process is a clinical interaction based on mutual power, shared in order to attain some desirable therapeutic outcome. If a client chooses not to go into hypnosis for whatever reason, then he or she will not. The nature of the hypnotic process is always context-determined. Even the most responsive clients can refuse to follow the suggestion of a hypnotist if they choose to. Prior experience with hypnosis, good or bad, is not the sole determining factor of whether hypnosis is accomplished or not. The communication and relationship factors of the particular context where hypnosis is performed are the key variables that will help determine the outcome (Barber, 1991; Diamond, 1987).

MISCONCEPTION: ONE CAN BE HYPNOTIZED TO SAY OR DO SOMETHING AGAINST ONE'S WILL

This is one of the most hotly debated issues in the entire field of hypnosis. The capacity to influence people to do things against their will exists. There is little room for doubt that people can be manipulated negatively to do things seemingly inconsistent with the person's prior beliefs and attitudes. To put it simply, brainwashing and other untoward influences exist. However, the conditions necessary to effect such powerful influence do not typically surface in the therapeutic context. In other words, controlling a person is possible under certain conditions, but those conditions are not in and of themselves hypnosis, and they are quite far removed from the ethical and sensitive applications of hypnosis promoted in this book (Weitzenhoffer, 1989).

MISCONCEPTION: BEING HYPNOTIZED CAN BE HAZARDOUS TO YOUR HEALTH

This misconception is a strong one in raising people's fears. In fact, there is legitimate basis for concern about the use of hypnosis, but the concern should not be about the experience of hypnosis harming anyone. Rather, the concern should be about *who* practices hypnosis and *how* it is practiced. Hypnosis itself is not harmful, but an incompetent or unethical practitioner *can* do some damage through sheer ignorance about the complexity of each person's mind or through a lack of respect for the integrity of each human being (Frauman, Lynn & Brentar, 1993; Kleinhauz & Eli, 1987; MacHovec, 1986).

In terms of potential emotional harm, it is *not* hypnosis itself that may cause damage; difficulties may arise due to either the content of a session or the clinician's inability to effectively guide the client. The same conditions exist, of course, in *any* helping relationship where one person is in distress, vulnerable, and seeking relief. An inexperienced or uneducated helper may inadvertently (rarely, if ever, is it intentional) offer poor advice, state misinformation as fact, make grandiose promises, misdiagnose a problem or its dynamics, or do nothing at all and simply waste the client's time and money.

The flipside of this issue and the reason for developing skills in hypnotic techniques is the considerable emotional good that effective hypnosis can generate. Through its ability to increase people's feelings of self-control and, thus, their self-confidence, hypnosis can be a powerful means for resolving emotional problems and enhancing emotional well-being. It is essential that the clinician have enough knowledge and skill to use it toward that end, for it is evident that *anything that has an ability to help has an ability to hurt.*

MISCONCEPTION: ONE INEVITABLY BECOMES DEPENDENT ON THE HYPNOTIST

Hypnosis as a therapeutic tool does not in and of itself foster dependency of any kind any more than other clinical tools such as a behavioral contract, analytical free association, or an intelligence test can. Dependency is a need, a reliance, that everyone has to *some* degree. To a greater or lesser extent, we all depend on others for things we feel are important to our well-being. In the helping professions, especially, people are seeking help at a time they are hurting and vulnerable. They depend on the clinician to help, to comfort, and to care. The clinician knows that one ultimate goal of treatment must be to help that person establish self-reliance and independence. Rather than foster dependence by indirectly encouraging the client to view the clinician as the source of answers to all of life's woes, hypnosis used properly can help the person in distress turn inwards in order to make use of the many experiences the person has acquired over his or her lifetime that can be used therapeutically. Consistent with the goal of self-reliance and use of personal power to help oneself is the teaching of self-hypnosis to those you work with (Alman & Lambrou, 1992; Fromm & Kahn, 1990; Sanders, 1991; Simpkins & Simpkins, 1991).

There is an old saying, "If you give a man a fish, you have given him a meal. If you teach him how to fish, you have given him a livelihood." Teaching self-hypnosis can allow for the emergence of a self-correcting mechanism that can assure those you work with that they *do* have greater control over their lives. It gives you an assurance that you have done your work well.

MISCONCEPTION: ONE CAN BECOME "STUCK" IN HYPNOSIS

Hypnosis is a state of focused attention, either inwardly or outwardly directed. It is controlled by the the client, who can initiate or terminate the experience any time he or she chooses (Kirsch, Lynn & Rhue, 1993; Watkins, 1986).

MISCONCEPTION: ONE IS ASLEEP OR UNCONSCIOUS WHEN IN HYPNOSIS

Hypnosis is *not* sleep! The experience of formally induced hypnosis resembles sleep from a physical standpoint (decreased activity, muscular relaxation, slowed breathing, etc.), but from a mental standpoint the client is relaxed yet alert. Ever-present is *some* level of awareness of current goings-on, even when the individual is in deeper states of hypnosis (Weitzenhoffer, 1989). In the case of informal, spontaneous hypnotic states, awareness is even more marked since physical relaxation need not be present.

Since hypnosis is not sleep, and even the client in deep hypnosis is oriented to external reality to some degree, the use of archaic phrases like "sleep deeply" are not relevant to the client's experience, and so should not be used.

MISCONCEPTION: HYPNOSIS ALWAYS INVOLVES A MONOTONOUS RITUAL OF INDUCTION

When you consider the communication aspects of hypnosis, you can appreciate that hypnosis occurs to some degree whenever someone turns his or her attention to and focuses on the ideas and feelings triggered by the communications of the guide. For as long as your attention is directed in an absorbing way, either inwardly on some subjective experience or outwardly on some external stimulus (which, in turn, creates an internal experience), you are in hypnosis to some degree.

Hypnosis does not have to be formally induced to occur. Likewise, the various classical hypnotic phenomena can (and do) occur routinely outside of formal hypnotic experience (Kirsch & Council, 1992). Communication has conditioning properties, and whether used in the form of a monotonous ritual induction or in the form of an offhand remark, it has the capacity to influence others' experience, and thus be hypnotic in effect.

MISCONCEPTION: ONE MUST BE RELAXED IN ORDER TO BE IN HYPNOSIS

Hypnosis has been described as a state of concentrated attention, one that varies in intensity according to individual and contextual characteristics. Also mentioned earlier was the idea that hypnosis can spontaneously develop while you are conversing, reading, and in countless other instances where your attention becomes fixed. You can be anxious, even in deep suspense, and still be focused, as in "glued to a mystery." Thus, physical relaxation is *not* a necessary prerequisite for hypnosis to occur (Banyai, Zseni & Tury, 1993; Malott, 1984).

MISCONCEPTION: HYPNOSIS IS A THERAPY

Hypnosis is *not* a therapy. Rather, it is a therapeutic tool that can be used in an infinite variety of ways. Hypnosis is not aligned with any one theoretical or practical orientation. In a larger sense, hypnosis is a part of every psychotherapy, and for that matter, a part of every interaction in which one person engages and influences another (Kirsch, Lynn & Rhue, 1993; Lankton, 1982).

MISCONCEPTION: HYPNOSIS MAY BE USED TO ACCURATELY RECALL EVERYTHING THAT HAS EVER HAPPENED TO YOU

There is a great need for clinicians to understand how memory works in order to best address this most important aspect of the individual. Some have compared the mind to a computer in which every memory is accurately stored and available for eventual retrieval. The computer metaphor is an inaccurate one, however. *The mind does not simply take in experience and store it in exact form for accurate recall later.* In fact, memories are stored on the basis of perceptions, and so are subject to many of the same distortions as perceptions. People can "remember" things that did not actually happen, they can remember selected fragments of an experience, and they can take bits and pieces of multiple memories and combine them into one false memory (McConkey, 1992; Orne, 1984; Yapko, 1994). This topic is at the heart of a raging debate now bitterly dividing the mental health profession. I will address this issue in greater depth in a later chapter.

CLOSURE ON MISCONCEPTIONS

How you conceptualize hypnosis and the mind will determine almost entirely what limits you place on your use of hypnosis, as well as what limits you will place on your clients. You are urged to give careful thought to the ways in which you think about hypnosis as a tool in treatment, and to review the literature available to help you clarify your beliefs.

REFERENCES

Alman, B. & Lambrou, P. (1992). *Self-hypnosis: The complete manual for health and self-change* (2nd ed.). New York: Brunner/Mazel.

Araoz, D. (1985). *The new hypnosis.* New York: Brunner/Mazel.

Banyai, E., Zseni, A. & Tury, F. (1993). Active-alert hypnosis in psychotherapy. In J. Rhue, S. Lynn & I. Kirsch (Eds.), *Handbook of clinical hypnosis* (pp. 271–290). Washington, DC: American Psychological Association.

Barber, J. (1980). Hypnosis and the unhypnotizable. *American Journal of Clinical Hypnosis, 23,* 4–9.

Barber, J. (1991). The locksmith model: Accessing hypnotic responsiveness. In S. Lynn & J. Rhue (Eds.), *Theories of hypnosis: Current models and perspectives* (pp. 241–274). New York: Guilford.

Diamond, M. (1987). The interactional basis of hypnotic experience: On the relational dimensions of hypnosis. *International Journal of Clinical and Experimental Hypnosis, 35*, 95–115.

Erickson, M. & Rossi, E. (1979). *Hypnotherapy: An exploratory casebook.* New York: Irvington.

Frauman, D., Lynn, S. & Brentar, J. (1993). Prevention and therapeutic management of "negative effects" in hypnotherapy. In J. Rhue, S. Lynn & I. Kirsch (Eds.), *Handbook of clinical hypnosis* (pp. 95–120). Washington, DC: American Psychological Association.

Fromm, E. & Kahn, S. (1990). *Self-hypnosis: The Chicago paradigm.* New York: Guilford.

Gilligan, S. (1982). Ericksonian approaches to clinical hypnosis. In J. Zeig (Ed.), *Ericksonian approaches to hypnosis and psychotherapy* (pp. 87–103). New York: Brunner/Mazel.

Gilligan, S. (1987). *Therapeutic trances: The cooperation principle in Ericksonian hypnotherapy.* New York: Brunner/Mazel.

Golden, W. (1986). Another view of choosing inductions. In B. Zilbergeld, M. Erickson & D. Araoz (Eds.), *Hypnosis: Questions and answers* (pp. 110–117). New York: Norton.

Grinder, J. & Bandler, R. (1981). *Trance-formations: Neuro-Linguistic Programming and the structure of hypnosis.* Moab, UT: Real People Press.

Haley, J. (1963). *Strategies of psychotherapy.* New York: Grune & Stratton.

Kirsch, I. & Council, J. (1992). Situational and personality correlates of hypnotic responsiveness. In E. Fromm & M. Nash (Eds.), *Contemporary hypnosis research* (pp. 267–291). New York: Guilford.

Kirsch, I., Lynn, S. & Rhue, J. (1993). Introduction to clinical hypnosis. In J. Rhue, S. Lynn & J. Kirsch (Eds.), *Handbook of clinical hypnosis* (pp. 3–22). Washington, DC: American Psychological Association.

Kleinhauz, M. & Eli, I. (1987). Potential deleterious effects of hypnosis in the clinical setting. *American Journal of Clinical Hypnosis, 29*, 3, 155–159.

Kroger, W. (1977). *Clinical and experimental hypnosis* (2nd ed.). Philadelphia: Lippincott.

Lankton, S. (1982). The occurrence and use of trance phenomena in nonhypnotic therapies. In J. Zeig (Ed.), *Ericksonian approaches to hypnosis and psychotherapy* (pp. 132–143). New York: Brunner/Mazel.

MacHovec, F. (1986). *Hypnosis complications: Prevention and risk management.* Springfield, IL: C.C. Thomas.

Malott, J. (1984). Active-alert hypnosis: Replication and extension of previous research. *Journal of Abnormal Psychology, 93*, 246–249.

McConkey, K. (1992). The effects of hypnotic procedures on remembering: The experimental findings and their implication for forensic hypnosis. In E. Fromm & M. Nash (Eds.), *Contemporary hypnosis research* (pp. 405–426). New York: Guilford.

Orne, M. (1984). The use and misuse of hypnosis in court. In W. Wester & A. Smith (Eds.), *Clinical hypnosis: A multidisciplinary approach* (pp. 497–524). Philadelphia: Lippincott.

Sanders, S. (1991). *Clinical self-hypnosis: The power of words and images.* New York: Guilford.

Simpkins, C. & Simpkins, A. (1991). *Principles of self-hypnosis: Pathways to the unconscious.* New York: Irvington.

Spiegel, H. & Spiegel, D. (1987). *Trance and treatment: Clinical uses of hypnosis.* Washington, DC: American Psychiatric Press.

Stanton, H. (1985). Permissive vs. authoritarian approaches in clinical and experimental settings. In J. Zeig (Ed.), *Ericksonian psychotherapy, Vol. 1: Structures* (pp. 293–304). New York: Brunner/Mazel.

Watkins, H. (1986). Handling a patient who doesn't come out of trance. In B. Zilbergeld, M. Edelstein & D. Araoz (Eds.), *Hypnosis: Questions and answers* (pp. 445–447). New York: Norton.

Weitzenhoffer, A. (1989). *The practice of hypnotism* (Vols. 1&2). New York: John Wiley & Sons.

Yapko, M. (1994). *Suggestions of abuse: True and false memories of childhood sexual trauma.* New York: Simon & Schuster.

5

HYPNOSIS, THEORETICALLY SPEAKING

How you conceptualize hypnosis has profound implications for its potential applications. Over the past few decades, there have been many perspectives, often differing sharply, on what the mysterious force called "hypnosis" is all about.

Each of the theories of hypnosis developed over the years is useful in describing one or more aspects of hypnosis, but none can be considered the final word in describing either the process or the experience of hypnosis. The following are some of the most prominent models and perspectives of hypnosis.

1. *Hypnosis as dissociation.* The underlying assumption is that there are multiple cognitive systems which normally work synergistically under the control of a primary or executive control. During hypnosis, the normally integrated subsystems dissociate from one another to various degrees and are thus capable of independent and multi-level responses to the suggestions of the hypnotist (Bowers & Davidson, 1991; Evans, 1991; Hilgard, 1977, 1979, 1986, 1991).
2. *Hypnosis as psychological regression.* Hypnosis is viewed as a special form of psychological regression characterized by a shift to more primitive primary-process thinking and increased transference to the hypnotist as an almost archetypal authority (i.e., parental) figure (Fromm, 1992; Nash, 1987).
3. *Hypnosis as relaxation.* Relaxation is considered the source from which all hypnotic phenomena, like regression and dissociation, are derived (Edmonston, 1977, 1981, 1991).

4. *Hypnosis as a sociocognitive phenomenon.* Sociocognitive perspectives hold that hypnosis is not a particular or unique experience, but is defined only by the social context in which it is evident and through the manner in which responses are deemed hypnotic by participants who label it as such (Kirsch, 1991; Spanos, 1991a, 1991b; Wagstaff, 1991).

5. *Hypnosis as a permissive state.* The authoritarian approach of most traditionally oriented clinicians is the basis for this theory's description of the demeanor of the client as a passive, permissive one. Specifically, a permissive client is characterized as one who permits the clinician to direct his or her experience, expressing little or no will of his or her own. The client is expected to respond as completely as possible to the guidance of the clinician, thus operating in a secondary, reactive role in the relationship. In essence, the client has been viewed as a passive receptacle for the authoritarian clinician's suggestions. An inability of the client to respond to the clinician's direct suggestions to the clinician's satisfaction is the basis for what has been deemed "resistance" in this model (Weitzenhoffer, 1989).

6. *Hypnosis as role playing.* There is a considerable amount of confusion and speculation over whether there really is a condition of human experience that can be called "hypnosis." Graphs of brain waves, measurements of biochemical changes in the body, and objective readings on the activity of the nervous system are ambiguous at best in helping to define the phenomenon. The nature of hypnosis is extremely subjective and, to date, has been resistant to objective measurements. Thus, there are some theorists (Coe & Sarbin, 1991; Sarbin & Coe, 1972) who have adopted a particular sociocognitive perspective suggesting that hypnosis as a separate and unique entity of consciousness does not really exist at all. In their view, there is hypnosis only when someone is willing to role-play it. In other words, the client does not actually enter a dimension of consciousness that differs appreciably from any other. Rather, the person plays the role of what a hypnotized subject is supposed to look and act like, and carries out the hypnotist's suggestions on that basis.

Support for this perspective comes from a variety of research, typically involving a group of subjects who are instructed to behave "as if" they were hypnotized and mixed with a group of subjects who were formally hypnotized. A number of "experts" in hypnosis were challenged to discover which individuals were and were not truly hypnotized. Subjects who role-played hypnotic behavior were extremely convincing and were able to successfully confound the experts.

7.   *Hypnosis as an altered state of consciousness.* The experience of hypnosis has also been conceptualized as an altered state of consciousness (Fromm, 1992; Tart, 1969). In this perspective, the hypnotic state is considered to be a unique and separate state of consciousness relative to one's "normal" state of consciousness. In this view, hypnosis is a state that is artificially created by the induction process, which alters the person's phenomenological experience through the narrowing of attention to the offered suggestions.

This view has historically been a popular one because of its recognition that people in hypnosis can experience things beyond their usual capacity. The idea of an altered state of consciousness allows for that possibility, and also allows for the variable proportion of people who can experience such a state as described in susceptibility statistics.

The key question, then, is this: If hypnosis is an altered state of consciousness, what is it altered *from*? Clearly, the state that arises from formal hypnotic interaction in which a hypnotized person experiences his or her body as numb, for example, is not an everyday experience. Clearly, *something* has changed, but what? And how? This remains a mystery. It was pointed out earlier that attempts to objectively measure the existence of the hypnotic state on chemical and electrical levels have been less than successful. Thus, a related view of hypnosis has emerged, namely that of the naturalistic, everyday dimensions of the hypnotic experience (Erickson & Rossi, 1979; Zeig, 1991).

8.   *The reality-testing view of hypnosis.* Obtaining feedback from our senses about our relationship to the world around us is a process commonly called "reality-testing." This process is generally so unconscious we take it for granted.

The reality-testing view of hypnosis theorizes that when you first enter and are then in hypnosis, your ongoing process of reality-testing is markedly reduced. When you suspend the process of obtaining feedback from the world around you by focusing inwardly, as is characteristic of most hypnotic experiences (although hypnosis can also be externally focused), you are no longer oriented to much of anything beyond your internal experience. By suspending objective reality-testing, it frees you to accept whatever reality is suggested to you. The suggested reality, like *any* believed-in reality, whether true or false, will determine the quantity and quality of your behavioral and emotional responses (Lynn & Rhue, 1991; Shor, 1959).

9. *The conditioning property of words and experiences.* You are reading this book, this page with lots of black inkmarks in various configurations. The patterns of configuration form what you have come to recognize (from years of learning and experience) as words. As you read each word in a fixed left-to-right sequence, you are taking the words and attaching them to your experience of what they mean to you. The words on this page don't mean anything at all to you *until* you attach a meaning to them, and the meaning can come only from your own experience of having learned what experience the words represent.

    The important point is that *you use your own individual experience in attaching meaning to a word.* Therefore, the same word will inevitably mean different things to different people. The more abstract a word, the more this is true.

    Words are conditioned stimuli representing internal experience. Gestures are also conditioned stimuli arising from repeated experiences of learning what they mean. The words and gestures mean whatever the person has become conditioned to believe they mean. Thus, meaning is in the person *not* the words. People are individuals, each communicating in his or her own way. Thus, effective hypnotic communication allows people to interpret and respond in their own unique ways to the possibilities suggested by the clinician (Bandler & Grinder, 1975, 1979; Grinder & Bandler, 1976; Lankton, 1979).

10. *Hypnosis as an interactional outcome.* In more traditional methods of hypnosis, the induction of hypnosis was something a hypnotist "did to" a subject. In a standardized, nonindividualized approach, inducing hypnosis was something a subject did to himself or herself in response to the impersonal approach of the hypnotist's suggestions. In the utilization approach, responsibility for the experience of hypnosis is a shared one between clinician and client in the sense that they must be attentive and responsive to each other. The clinician, to be successful, must be responsive to the needs of the client and tailor his or her approaches to those needs in order for the client to be responsive to the possibilities for change the clinician suggests. The relationship is one of mutual interdependence, each following the other's leads while, paradoxically, at the same time leading (Erickson & Rossi, 1979; Erickson, Rossi & Rossi, 1976; Zeig, 1991).

The interactional view emphasizes responsiveness and respect for the client, which is ideal in therapeutic contexts. However, clearly these factors need not be present for hypnosis to occur. After all, the performing stage hypnotist has no special personal relationship to his or her subjects, and is certainly not sensitive or responsive to their unique personal characteristics and personalities.

11. *Biological views of hypnosis.* The strong relationship between mind and body clearly evident in hypnotically-based interactions has led to theoretical formulations of a biological basis for or predisposition to hypnosis. Spiegel & Spiegel (1987) described the quality of the interrelationship of the two brain hemispheres as the basis for hypnotic responsiveness. Rossi (1982, 1991) postulated a natural biological cycle of alternating attentiveness and relaxation that physiologically occurs about every 90 to 150 minutes as a component of the body's 24-hour cycle (called the circadian rhythm). The "ultradian rhythm" of alternating attentiveness and relaxation is viewed as the biological framework for the hypnotic state. Watzlawick (1978) described hypnosis as a product of hemispheric asymmetry, suggesting that the induction of hypnosis distracts the left hemisphere (i.e., the "rational" part) while the right hemisphere's impressionistic and intuitive processes become dominant in one's experience.

REFERENCES

Bandler, R. & Grinder, J. (1975). *The structure of magic* (Vol. 1). Palo Alto, CA: Science and Behavior Books.

Bandler, R. & Grinder, J. (1979). *Frogs into princes*. Moab, UT: Real People Press.

Bowers, K. & Davidson, T. (1991). A neodissociative critique of Spanos social-psychological model of hypnosis. In S. Lynn & J. Rhue (Eds.), *Theories of hypnosis: Current models and perspectives* (pp. 105–143). New York: Guilford.

Coe, W. & Sarbin, T. (1991). Role theory: Hypnosis from a dramaturigical and narrational perspective. In S. Lynn & J. Rhue (Eds.), *Theories of hypnosis: Current models and perspectives* (pp. 303–323). New York: Guilford.

Edmonston, W. (1977). Neutral hypnosis as relaxation. *American Journal of Clinical Hypnosis, 20*, 69–75.

Edmonston, W. (1981). *Hypnosis and relaxation: Modern verification of an old equation*. New York: John Wiley & Sons.

Edmonston, W. (1991). Anesis. In S. Lynn & J. Rhue (Eds.), *Theories of hypnosis: Current models and perspectives* (pp. 197–237). New York: Guilford.

Erickson, M. & Rossi, E. (1979). *Hypnotherapy: An exploratory casebook*. New York: Irvington.

Erickson, M., Rossi, E. & Rossi, S. (1976). *Hypnotic realities: The induction of clinical hypnosis and forms of indirect suggestion.* New York: Irvington.

Evans, F. (1991). Hypnotizability: Individual differences in dissociation and the flexible control of psychological processes. In S. Lynn & J. Rhue (Eds.), *Theories of hypnosis: Current models and perspectives* (pp. 144–168). New York: Guilford.

Fromm, E. (1992). An ego-psychological theory of hypnosis. In E. Fromm & M. Nash (Eds.), *Contemporary hypnosis research* (pp. 132–148). New York: Guilford.

Grinder, J. & Bandler, R. (1976). *The structure of magic* (Vol. 2). Palo Alto, CA: Science and Behavior Books.

Hilgard, E. (1977). *Divided consciousness.* New York: John Wiley & Sons.

Hilgard, E. (1979). Divided consciousness in hypnosis: The implications of the hidden observer. In E. Fromm & R. Shor (Eds.), *Hypnosis: Developments in research and new perspectives* (2nd ed.) (pp. 45–79). Chicago: Aldine Atherton.

Hilgard, E. (1986). *Divided consciousness: Multiple controls in human thought and action.* New York: John Wiley & Sons.

Hilgard, E. (1991). A neodissociation interpretation of hypnosis. In S. Lynn & J. Rhue (Eds.), *Theories of hypnosis: Current models and perspectives* (pp. 83–104). New York: Guilford.

Kirsch, I. (1991). The social learning theory of hypnosis. In S. Lynn & J. Rhue (Eds.), *Theories of hypnosis: Current models and perspectives* (pp. 439–465). New York: Guilford.

Lankton, S. (1979). *Practical magic: The clinical applications of Neuro-Linguistic Programming.* Cupertino, CA: Meta Publications.

Lynn, S. & Rhue, J. (1991). An integrative model of hypnosis. In S. Lynn & J. Rhue (Eds.), *Theories of hypnosis: Current models and perspectives* (pp. 397–438). New York: Guilford.

Nash, M. (1987). What, if anything, is regressed about hypnotic age regression? A review of the empirical literature. *Psychological Bulletin, 102,* 42–52.

Rossi, E. (1982). Hypnosis and ultradian cycles: A new state(s) theory of hypnosis? *American Journal of Clinical Hypnosis, 1,* 21–32.

Rossi, E. (1991). *The 20-minute break: Using the new science of ultradian rhythms.* Los Angeles: Tarcher.

Sarbin, T. & Coe, W. (1972). *Hypnosis: A social-psychological analysis of influence communication.* New York: Holt, Rinehart & Winston.

Shor, R. (1959). Hypnosis and the concept of the generalized reality-orientation. *American Journal of Psychotherapy, 13,* 582–602.

Spanos, N. (1991a). Hypnosis, hypnotizability and hypnotherapy. In C. Snyder (Ed.), *Handbook of social and clinical psychology.* Elmsford, NY: Pergamon.

Spanos, N. (1991b). A sociocognitive approach to hypnosis. In S. Lynn & J. Rhue (Eds.), *Theories of hypnosis: Current models and perspectives* (pp. 324–361). New York: Guilford.

Spiegel, H. & Spiegel, D. (1987). *Trance and treatment: Clinical uses of hypnosis.* Washington, DC: American Psychiatric Press.

Tart, C. (Ed.) (1969). *Altered states of consciousness: A book of readings.* New York:

John Wiley & Sons.

Wagstaff, G. (1991). Compliance, belief, and semantics in hypnosis: A nonstate, sociocognitive perspective. In S. Lynn & J. Rhue (Eds.), *Theories of hypnosis: Current models and perspectives* (pp. 362–369). New York: Guilford.

Watzlawick, P. (1978). *The language of change.* New York: Basic Books.

Weitzenhoffer, A. (1989). *The practice of hypnotism* (Vols. 1&2). New York: John Wiley & Sons.

Zeig, J. (1991). Ericksonian hypnotherapy: A communications approach to hypnosis. In S. Lynn & J. Rhue (Eds.), *Theories of hypnosis: Current models and perspectives* (pp. 275–300). New York: Guilford.

6

CONTEXTS OF HYPNOSIS

I am often asked, "Can hypnosis be used for (fill-in-the-blank)?" My response is to promote the idea that hypnosis can be used as a tool in the treatment of *any* human condition in which a person's attitude is a factor.

Wherever there is involvement of the person's mind in a particular problem, which is *everywhere* to one degree or another as far as I can tell, there is some potential gain to be made through the application of hypnotic patterns. With that point in mind, let us consider specific contexts where the tool of hypnosis may be used to facilitate desired outcomes.

MEDICAL HYPNOSIS

In general, hypnosis can be a useful adjunct to more traditional medical treatments for several reasons, the first of which relates to the mind-body relationship and the role of the mind (attitudes and related emotions) in medical disorders (Barber, 1984; Cohen & Williamson, 1991; Levenson & Bemis, 1991).

A second reason for making use of hypnosis is its emphasis, by its very nature, on the responsibility of each person for his or her own health and well-being. Use of hypnosis gives people a direct experience of having some control over their internal experiences (Brown, 1992; Brown & Fromm, 1987).

Specific applications of hypnosis in medical contexts are greatly varied, but can generally be described as a way of attaining a significant degree of control over physical processes. One possibility is the reduction or elimination of pain without the use of medication (Chaves, 1993; Spanos, 1989).

Methods of hypnotic pain management are generally very sophisticated, and you are advised to have a very strong background of education and experience in hypnosis before working with such cases. Working with patients in pain presupposes appropriate medical licensure or, at least, appropriate medical supervision in *all* cases.

Hypnosis is commonly used in the treatment of stress disorders, and is considered to be a highly effective treatment. Teaching the medical patient techniques for preventing negative stress wherever possible, techniques for identifying stress well before it reaches a level where it is likely to cause debilitating symptoms, and techniques for relaxing and managing stress positively are all elements in teaching a hypertensive patient to manage his or her condition positively and responsibly (Hammond, 1990).

Hypnosis in the treatment of serious diseases, as an adjunct, not a replacement, for more traditional approaches, has demonstrated the necessity of addressing the patient's emotional needs while using his or her mental resources as an integral part of treatment. This is true even for diseases that seem, and probably are, entirely organic in nature. The exact mechanism whereby a clinician can utter a few hypnotic phrases and effect changes in the patient is unknown, but the answer is thought to reside in the immunological system of the person. Current research in this area suggests that people are more likely to develop a serious disease during or soon after a highly stressful period in their lives. Stress is thought to reduce the capacity of the body's natural defenses, the immunological system, allowing disease organisms to multiply in the weakened person. Hypnosis is thought to be able to strengthen the body's immunological functions and assist in fighting off the disease (Rossi, 1993; Wickramasekera, 1993).

Much research needs to be done to discover solutions to the mysteries of the mind, but the lack of precise explanations for mechanisms of action should not inhibit the use of techniques that clearly can assist in the healing of a human body. Hypnosis can facilitate the recovery process, and can be another useful tool in the physician's repertoire to share with his or her patients. Hypnosis doesn't replace other treatments—it adds to them.

DENTAL HYPNOSIS

The powerful mind-body relationship evidenced in medical applications of hypnosis can also be applied in the dental context.

Helping a patient reduce his or her anxiety about receiving dental treatment with a few well-chosen statements can make a huge difference in the outcome. Furthermore, one good dental experience can skillfully be used as a prototype for future dental experiences. The person may not eagerly await the next appointment, but he or she won't have to live in dread either (Finkelstein, 1984, 1991; Hammond, 1990).

A second good use of hypnosis in dentistry involves the use of pain management techniques. Hypnotic techniques for creating the experience of analgesia or anesthesia can allow the patient to reduce the degree of discomfort to a more easily managed level. Many are able to eliminate the discomfort altogether.

A third use of hypnosis in dentistry is for its ability to assist in directing the flow of blood. Many patients can respond to suggestions to reduce the flow of blood to the area under treatment. The result is a less traumatic experience for the patient and greater clarity for the dentist in seeing what he or she is doing (Banks, 1985).

Another use of hypnosis in the dental context is for the enhancement of the healing process following treatment. Use of hypnosis techniques involving the imagining of healing (e.g., images, feelings, and sounds associated with rebuilding, repairing, and strengthening) can both shorten the recovery period and allow greater comfort during that time (Rossi & Cheek, 1988).

HYPNOSIS IN THE FORENSIC SCIENCES

As of this writing, the use of hypnotically obtained testimony has been severely curtailed in the courtroom (Scheflin & Shapiro, 1989). Experts are at odds over the issue of such testimony because of the known ability to contaminate memories through hypnosis and suggestion. Some experts hold that the information obtained from a hypnotized person is as usable and reliable as any other information, and that hypnosis does not necessarily distort memory. On the other side of the issue are those who claim that hypnosis can alter memory, and that the hypnotized witness can easily lie while in hypnosis, and is likely to fill in missing details either with fantasy material or with information contained in the subtle leading questions of the investigator (Sheehan & McConkey, 1993; Yapko, 1994). This issue is addressed further in a later chapter.

HYPNOSIS IN EDUCATION

Teaching and learning are highly refined skills that require a great amount of information processing on multiple levels. Teaching is a learning experience—learning how to capture students' interest and attention (a skill also necessary for the induction of hypnosis), learning how to present information in such a way that the student can use it (a skill also necessary for utilizing the hypnotic state), and learning how to allow students to become self-sufficient learners (a skill necessary for consolidating therapy results), so they may be competent and motivated to learn in the absence of the teacher. Whether a teacher is teaching preschoolers or doctoral candidates, effective teaching involves these steps which closely parallel hypnotic patterns.

Many creative teachers at all levels are using hypnosis in their teaching, often guiding students with formal relaxation and imagery procedures, for example. Many students are developing study skills with self-hypnosis exercises, learning to manage anxiety better and to increase their ability to pay attention to and organize their subject of study. Hypnosis in the educational context, whether formally or informally used, can enhance both teaching skills and student performance (Stanton, 1993; Wolf, 1986).

HYPNOSIS IN BUSINESS

In the business context, formal hypnosis (the use of overt hypnotic induction procedures) is less applicable than is the use of informal patterns of suggestion. Communication that influences is the guiding definition of hypnosis in this book; in the business context, the principles of effective communication can either make or break a company.

For the businessperson who is able to communicate his or her ideas in clear and flexible ways to others, there is a greater likelihood of success at all levels. Interactions such as the presentation of a marketing plan, the strategic handling of a troublesome employee or supervisor, the effective job interview, conducting meaningful performance evaluations, clarifying job expectations, creating a better work atmosphere, and handling the many other dimensions of the business world all ultimately involve interpersonal interactions where communication and influence inevitably occur. The issue is not one of whether one communicates and influences, which is impossible *not* to do, but rather one of whether the communication patterns that exist influence participants in a desirable way (Alman & Lambrou, 1992; Korn, Pratt & Lambrou, 1987).

HYPNOSIS IN SPORTS

Engaging in athletics with any degree of intensity involves a large measure of physical control and mental concentration. Hypnosis as a tool can facilitate both with increased efficiency.

In addition to building concentration and physical control, hypnosis can help in better managing the tension or self-doubts inherent in competing. Furthermore, building positive expectations and positive communication with yourself through self-hypnosis can enhance your performance dramatically. Often, the troubled slumping athlete has mental images of failure, which can all too easily get translated into real failure. Building positive images through hypnosis and self-hypnosis can turn an athlete's performance around completely. Certainly, hypnosis does not provide extra talent to the athlete; it simply amplifies the talent the athlete already has, giving him or her access to as much of his or her talent as possible. A lot of athletes appreciate that, as you can well imagine (Liggett & Hamada, 1993; Masters, 1992; Morgan, 1993; Ward, 1992).

HYPNOSIS AND PSYCHOTHERAPY

Every psychotherapy involves influencing a troubled person in some way so the person may feel better. The client seeking psychotherapy cannot *not* respond to your communications; the sophistication of a good therapist is getting a desired, therapeutic response.

Hypnosis is a tool, not a therapy. The main advantage of using hypnosis in psychotherapy lies in its ability to draw upon the many resources of the unconscious mind. Feelings, values, behaviors, memories, and understandings, all the perceptions that guide the client's choices, are subjective and thus can change. Hypnosis that involves simply inducing hypnosis formally and then giving suggestions directly related to the problem is the most superficial and least sophisticated use of hypnosis. This kind of hypnosis is used on a symptomatic basis, and is practiced by almost all lay hypnotists and even by many psychotherapists. Despite its superficiality, it can still be effective with a considerable percentage of individuals.

More complex and more skilled use of hypnosis involves the use of techniques aimed at resolution of deeper conflicts (taking the symptoms with them or else it is not truly a success). This kind of hypnosis involves more of an interactional approach and works on multiple dimensions of the individual, not just on the most superficial ones.

The flexibility of hypnosis as a tool of psychotherapy allows clinicians to use it as superficially or as intensively as deemed appropriate in whatever disorder is being treated. Hypnotic methods continually remind us that experience is negotiable (Araoz, 1985; Brown, 1991; Crasilneck & Hall, 1985; Erickson & Rossi, 1979, 1981; Hammond, 1990;

O'Hanlon, 1987; Rossi, 1980; Spiegel & Spiegel, 1987; Zeig, 1982, 1985; Zeig & Lankton, 1988).

REFERENCES

Alman, B. & Lambrou, P. (1992). *Self-hypnosis: The complete manual for health and self-change.* New York: Brunner/Mazel.

Araoz, D. (1985). *The new hypnosis.* New York: Brunner/Mazel.

Banks, W. (1985). Hypnotic suggestion for the control of bleeding in the angiography suite. *Ericksonian Monographs, 1,* 76–88.

Barber, T. (1984). Changing unchangeable bodily processes by hypnotic suggestions: A new look at hypnosis, cognitions, imagining and the mind-body problem. *Advances 1,* 2, 7–40.

Brown, D. (1992). Clinical hypnosis research since 1986. In E. Fromm & M. Nash (Eds.), *Contemporary hypnosis research* (pp. 427–458). New York: Guilford.

Brown, D. & Fromm, E. (1987). *Hypnosis and behavioral medicine.* Hillsdale, NJ: Erlbaum.

Brown, P. (1991). *The hypnotic brain.* New Haven, CT: Yale University Press.

Chaves, J. (1993). Hypnosis in pain management. In J. Rhue, S. Lynn & I. Kirsch (Eds.), *Handbook of clinical hypnosis* (pp. 511–532). Washington, DC: American Psychological Association.

Cohen, S. & Williamson, G. (1991). Stress and infectious disease in humans. *Psychological Bulletin, 108,* 5–24.

Crasilneck, H. & Hall, J. (1985). *Clinical hypnosis: Principles and applications* (2nd ed.). New York: Grune & Stratton.

Erickson, M. & Rossi, E. (1979). *Hypnotherapy: An exploratory casebook.* New York: Irvington.

Erickson, M. & Rossi, E. (1981). *Experiencing hypnosis: Therapeutic approaches to altered states.* New York: Irvington.

Finkelstein, S. (1984). Hypnosis and dentistry. In W. Wester & A. Smith (Eds.), *Clinical hypnosis: A multidisciplinary approach* (pp. 337–352). Philadelphia: Lippincott.

Finkelstein, S. (1991). Hypnotically assisted preparation of the anxious patient for medical and dental treatment. *American Journal of Clinical Hypnosis, 33,* 3, 187–191.

Hammond, D. (Ed.) (1990). *Handbook of hypnotic suggestions and metaphors.* New York: Norton.

Korn, E., Pratt, G. & Lambrou, P. (1987). *Hyper-performance: The A.I.M. strategy for releasing your business potential.* New York: John Wiley & Sons.

Levenson, J. & Bemis, C. (1991). The role of psychological factors in cancer onset and progression. *Psychosomatics, 32,* 124–132.

Liggett, D. & Hamada, S. (1993). Enhancing the visualization of gymnasts. *American Journal of Clinical Hypnosis, 35,* 3, 190–197.

Masters, K. (1992). Hypnotic susceptibility, cognitive dissociation, and runner's high in a sample of marathon runners. *American Journal of Clinical Hypnosis, 34,* 3, 193–201.

Morgan, W. (1993). Hypnosis and sport psychology. In J. Rhue, S. Lynn & I. Kirsch (Eds.), *Handbook of clinical hypnosis* (pp. 649–670). Washington, DC: American Psychological Association.

O'Hanlon, W. (1987). *Taproots.* New York: Norton.

Rossi, E. (Ed.) (1980). *The collected papers of Milton H. Erickson on hypnosis* (Vols. 1–4). New York: Irvington.

Rossi, E. (1993). *The psychobiology of mind-body healing* (Rev. ed.). New York: Norton.

Rossi, E. & Cheek, D. (1988). *Mind-body therapy: Metaphors of ideodynamic healing in hypnosis.* New York: Norton.

Scheflin, A. & Shapiro, J. (1989). *Trance on trial.* New York: Guilford.

Sheehan, P. & McConkey, K. (1993). Forensic hypnosis: The application of ethical guidelines. In J. Rhue, S. Lynn & I. Kirsch (Eds.), *Handbook of clinical hypnosis* (pp. 719–738). Washington, DC: American Psychological Association.

Spanos, N. (1989). Experimental research on hypnotic analgesia. In N. Spanos & J. Chaves (Eds.), *Hypnosis: The cognitive-behavioral perspective* (pp. 206–240). Buffalo, NY: Prometheus Books.

Spiegel, H. & Spiegel, D. (1987). *Trance and treatment: Clinical uses of hypnosis.* Washington, DC: American Psychiatric Press.

Stanton, H. (1993). Using hypnotherapy to overcome examination anxiety. *American Journal of Clinical Hypnosis, 35,* 3, 198–204.

Ward, W. (1992). Hypnosis, mental images, and "peer-coaching" in gymnasts. In W. Bongartz (Ed.), *Hypnosis 175 years after Mesmer* (pp. 451–460). Konstanz: Universitats Verlag.

Wickramasekera, I. (1993). Assessment and treatment of somatization disorders: The high risk model of threat perception. In J. Rhue, S. Lynn & I. Kirsch (Eds.), *Handbook of clinical hypnosis* (pp. 587–621). Washington DC: American Psychological Association.

Wolf, T. (1986). Hypnosis and Ericksonian interventions with children in the elementary school. In M. Yapko (Ed.), *Hypnotic and strategic interventions: Principles and practice* (pp. 209–214). New York: Irvington.

Wolinsky, S. (1991). *Trances people live.* Falls Village, CT: The Bramble Co.

Zeig, J. (Ed.) (1982). *Ericksonian approaches to hypnosis and psychotherapy.* New York: Brunner/Mazel.

Zeig, J. (Ed.) (1985). *Ericksonian psychotherapy* (Vols. 1&2). New York: Brunner/Mazel.

Zeig, J. & Lankton, S. (1988). *Developing Ericksonian therapy: State of the art.* New York: Brunner/Mazel.

7

HUMAN SUGGESTIBILITY

The field of social psychology offers a number of valuable insights into the dynamics of interpersonal influence relevant to the use of hypnosis. An individual's behavior changes in the presence of another individual, often in systematic and predictable ways (Cialdini, 1985; Sherman, 1988).

THE INFLUENCE OF ADVERTISING

Why do you buy the products you buy when you shop? How did you come to choose one brand over another?

Advertising as an industry makes great use of hypnotic techniques to influence you to buy a product. Advertisers begin by creating a need for a product (for many centuries, bad breath or body odor was not on the forefront of people's consciousness), using techniques such as promoting identification with the person in the ad so that you'll solve your problem by using the product in the same way he or she modeled it for you. Then they strengthen your buying habit by telling you how (bright, masculine, feminine, whatever) you are for having made such a fine choice. Ads try to generate feelings or recognitions that will be tied to the product, associations that will influence you to purchase one brand over another. The entire field of advertising uses words and images in a way that is intended to influence your buying behaviors. And it works!

What is suggestibility? It is an openness to accepting and responding to new ideas, new information. As this new information is acquired, depending on its subjective value, it can alter your experience anywhere from a little to a lot. In the therapy context, the client to be influenced is, to some unknown degree, suggestible; he or she wants to acquire some new information or experiences that will allow him or her to alleviate distress. The person is unhappy with some aspect of himself or herself, and seeks help from someone else who might be able to say or do

38

something to make a positive difference. Most people are not completely noncritical in accepting information, and so there is an appreciable difference between suggestibility and gullibility. Hypnosis does *not* make anyone gullible.

THE NEED FOR CLARITY AND CERTAINTY

The old saying, "When in Rome, do as the Romans do," reflects the reliance on other people as models of what to do when we are faced with uncertainty of what is proper behavior. These models can thus be powerful influences on us. A therapist will have some influence arising from the client's belief that he or she is mismanaging some portion of his or her life. The symptoms seem to be outside of his or her control. Previous attempts at self-correction have failed, and so the person may then seek out someone apparently more knowledgeable to learn from.

If you have attempted to change some habit pattern and failed (who hasn't?), you may accept the suggestion that someone who is professionally trained in such matters will be able to help you. The helping professional may be seen as an authority on treating personal problems because he or she has been trained to recognize causes and treatments. The person seeking help has already accepted his own ignorance and powerlessness about the situation, and with a strong sense of hopefulness, the therapist is looked to as the person who can make the hurt go away (Coe, 1993; Eisen, 1990).

THERAPIST POWER

When a person comes in for help to deal with a distressing problem, that person is making an investment in the therapist as a person of authority and, hopefully, a source of cure. Power is not typically something the therapist has in and of himself or herself; rather, it is an acquired property from the person's reaction to the therapist (Barber, 1991; Diamond, 1984; Strauss, 1993).

There are at least five different types of power: 1) coercive (derived from the ability to punish), 2) reward (derived from the ability to give benefits ranging from monetary to psychological), 3) legitimate (derived from position, including elected and selected positions), 4) expert (derived from greater knowledge in an area), and 5) referent power (derived from personal characteristics, such as likability or amiability). All five of these powers are operational in almost any context to one degree or another, but are especially prevalent in the therapeutic context. The role of therapist can be a powerful one. The capacity for influence in using principles and techniques of clinical hypnosis must lead you to consider the dimension of power in relationships carefully if you are to use power sensitively and with absolute respect for the integrity of the client (Aronson, 1992; Frauman, Lynn & Brentar, 1993).

THE NEED FOR ACCEPTANCE

The person seeking help or information is feeling deficient or incomplete in some way. A basic need people seem to have, which is the cornerstone of society, is for other people. When you combine the feeling of deficiency with the need for others, the need for acceptance begins to emerge. One of the largest fears in the mind of the typical client coming in for help is, "If I disclose myself to you, with all my fears, doubts, and imperfections, will you like me and accept me? Or will you find me weak, repulsive, and somehow less than human?" (Bates, 1993).

The need for acceptance and the need to belong are also factors present in the hypnotic relationship. Avoiding confrontations with the authority, doing things to please him or her (ranging from generating therapeutic results to knitting him or her a sweater) and conforming to the therapist's language style, values, and theoretical ideas are all ways this need can be discovered within the therapy relationship. Relative to the discussion on power, this is where reward power becomes a considerable force in the process.

EXPECTATIONS

The role of expectations on experience is a profound one that has been demonstrated in numerous places and been called by many names. Probably the most widely used term is "self-fulfilling prophecy," describing the likelihood that what we expect to happen will happen, and, conversely, what we don't expect to happen will not. (We unconsciously align our behavior with our expectations.)

The ideas that a person has about his or her future experiences will guide his present experiences in that direction. The more of an emotional investment the person has in that expectation, the less likely he or she is to experience anything that contradicts it (Coe, 1993; Torem, 1992; Zeig & Rennick, 1991).

THE NEED FOR INTERNAL HARMONY

Human beings generally have a desire to alleviate confusion and contradictions from within. They typically do so by omitting contradictory bits of information or by twisting information around until it all fits comfortably. People generally have a strong desire to feel certain, and when they are uncertain, perhaps because of the novelty or ambiguity of the situation, they often will turn to others to find out what is right. The more the explanation fits their personal needs, the more easily the explanation given is taken in at a deeper level (Festinger, 1957; Sherman, 1988).

For example, the need for cognitive consistency may surface, more or less depending on the individual, as a need to claim some benefit from having paid for and received professional help. When people invest money, hope, and time in something, they desperately want it to work, even if "only a little." They may have the need to justify their investment to themselves, converting a loser into a winner in order to feel better. This need is evident in the testimonials of people who have bought products that are virtually valueless, whose only benefit to them was derived from their own expectations.

Consider the role of expectations and the need for cognitive consistency when a client views himself or herself as a hopeless case, and will go to great lengths to try to prove it. The client who has been to every doctor in town and is proud of his or her inability to be helped is a perfect example; the client who spends years in psychotherapy going from therapist to therapist is another (Schoen, 1993).

CONCLUSION

There are no set rules about what makes for the most influential communication. What appeals to one person will not appeal to another. Some people appreciate and seek out professional help, others would rather seek out the advice of a friendly neighbor. Some people want to be told what to do in a step-by-step fashion and then they follow such directions happily; others fight such remedial directions and want to be left alone to figure things out for themselves. Some respond better if they have to go through demands to reach a goal (e.g., a therapist with a waiting list is a frustration to a new client who may then perceive that therapist as better when an appointment is finally obtained). Others won't even consider putting up with such demands (if faced with a waiting list, they'll just go see another therapist). Some require objective evidence for everything they hear, others are suspicious of science and of those who promote its methods. Some open up to the ideas of others when they feel confused,while others close off and resolve the confusion within themselves (even if with misinformation).

In order to be truly influential, discovering where (*not* whether) a person is open to suggestion (as most people are to *some* degree) is the task of the clinician. The suggestibility of each individual is what makes change possible and allows personal growth to take place. The process of discovering what your client wants and how to best reach him or her is the process of acquiring rapport, arising when your client senses that you have an understanding and empathy with his or her experience (Bertrand, 1989; Gfeller, 1993; Kirsch & Council, 1992; Sheehan, 1991).

REFERENCES

Aronson, E. (1992). *The social animal* (6th ed.). San Francisco: W.H. Freeman.

Barber, J. (1991). The locksmith model: Accessing hypnotic responsiveness. In S. Lynn & J. Rhue (Eds.), *Theories of hypnosis: Current models and perspectives* (pp. 241–274). New York: Guilford.

Bates, B. (1993). Individual differences in response to hypnosis. In J. Rhue, S. Lynn & I. Kirsch (Eds.), *Handbook of clinical hypnosis* (pp. 23–54). Washington, DC: American Psychological Association.

Bertrand, L. (1989). The assessment and modification of hypnotic susceptibility. In N. Spanos & J. Chaves (Eds.), *Hypnosis: The cognitive-behavioral perspective* (pp. 18–31). Buffalo, NY: Prometheus Books.

Cialdini, R. (1985). *Influence: Science and practice*. Glenview, IL: Scott, Foresman.

Coe, W. (1993). Expectations and hypnotherapy. In J. Rhue, S. Lynn & I. Kirsch (Eds.), *Handbook of clinical hypnosis* (pp. 73–93). Washington, DC: American Psychological Association.

Diamond, M. (1984). It takes two to tango: The neglected importance of the hypnotic relationship. *American Journal of Clinical Hypnosis, 26*, 1–13.

Eisen, M. (1990). From the magical wish to the belief in the self. In M. Fass & D. Brown (Eds.), Creative mastery in hypnosis and hypnoanalysis (pp. 147–157). Hillsdale, NJ: Erlbaum.

Festinger, L. (1957). *A theory of cognitive dissonance*. Stanford, CA: Stanford University Press.

Frauman, D., Lynn, J. & Brentar, J. (1993). Prevention and therapeutic management of "negative effects" in hypnotherapy. In J. Rhue, S. Lynn & I. Kirsch (Eds.), *Handbook of clinical hypnosis* (pp. 95–120). Washington, DC: American Psychological Association.

Gfeller, J. (1993). Enhancing hypnotizability and treatment responsiveness. In J. Rhue, S. Lynn & I. Kirsch (Eds.), *Handbook of clinical hypnosis* (pp. 235–250). Washington, DC: American Psychological Association.

Kirsch, I. (1990). *Changing expectations: A key to effective psychotherapy*. Pacific Grove, CA: Brooks/Cole.

Kirsch, I. & Council, J. (1992). Situational and personality correlates of hypnotic responsiveness. In E. Fromm & M. Nash (Eds.), *Contemporary hypnosis research* (pp. 267–291). New York: Guilford.

Schoen, M. (1993). Resistance to health: When the mind interferes with the desire to become well. *American Journal of Clinical Hypnosis, 36*, 1, 47–54.

Sheehan, P. (1991). Hypnosis, context, and commitment. In S. Lynn & J. Rhue

(Eds.), *Theories of hypnosis: Current models and perspectives* (pp. 520–541). New York: Guilford.

Sherman, S. (1988). Ericksonian psychotherapy and social psychology. In J. Zeig & S. Lankton (Eds.), *Developing Ericksonian therapy: State of the art* (pp. 59–90). New York: Brunner/Mazel.

Strauss, B. (1993). Operator variables in hypnotherapy. In J. Rhue, S. Lynn & I. Kirsch (Eds.), *Handbook of clinical hypnosis* (pp. 55–72). Washington, DC: American Psychological Association.

Torem, M. (1992). Back from the future: A powerful age-progression technique. *American Journal of Clinical Hypnosis, 35,* 2, 81–88.

Weitzenhoffer, A. (1989). *The practice of hypnotism* (Vols. 1&2). New York: John Wiley & Sons.

Zeig, J. & Rennick, P. (1991). Ericksonian hypnotherapy: A communications approach to hypnosis. In S. Lynn & J. Rhue (Eds.), *Theories of hypnosis: Current models and perspectives* (pp. 275–300). New York: Guilford.

8

MIND MATTERS

A most significant variable in determining the effectiveness of hypnotic communication is the way the conscious and unconscious minds respond to a message. The communications you are exposed to are experienced on a conscious level to some degree where they are processed in a fashion characteristic of conscious mind patterning. The same communications, however, are processed simultaneously on unconscious levels in a different fashion. In using hypnotic patterns, suggestions are deliberately formed in order to convey meaning to the client's unconscious mind while his or her conscious mind is preoccupied elsewhere. Acknowledging the differences between conscious and unconscious characteristics is immediately relevant to the formulation of effective suggestions (Hilgard, 1986; Kihlstrom, 1987; McConkey, 1991).

CONSCIOUS AND UNCONSCIOUS CHARACTERISTICS

The conscious and unconscious minds have some different functions, but also share a considerable number of functions between them. The overlap allows them to work together, while the differences can and often do surface in internal conflict and dissociated responses. The conscious mind is loosely defined as that part of the mind that allows you to be aware of things; whenever you pay attention to something or when you notice something, you are conscious of it. The things in your immediate awareness are in your conscious mind. The conscious mind has the ability to analyze things, to reason, and to make judgments about what is right or wrong. It is the conscious mind that very rationally (or so it rationalizes) decides what is possible to do and what is not possible to do. Consequently, the limitations in your life are, in part, limitations based on your conscious mind's critical appraisal of experience. Bypassing the client's conscious mind and its critical nature is fundamental to

44

successful utilization of the more complex hypnotic phenomena (Dixon & Laurence, 1992; Kihlstrom, 1984; Zeig, 1980).

The unconscious mind is that part of you that is a reservoir of all the experiences acquired throughout your lifetime. Your experience, learnings, manner (drives, motivations, needs) for interacting with your world, and your automatic functioning in countless behaviors each day are all evidence of unconscious functions. The unconscious mind is, in contrast to the conscious mind, not as rigid, analytical, and, most importantly, limited. It responds to experiential communications, is capable of symbolic interpretation, and tends to be more global in view (Brown, 1991; Ornstein, 1991).

UNCONSCIOUS PROCESSING

Just because a person is not aware of taking in information doesn't mean the person hasn't absorbed any. Information that is integrated at unconscious levels can be as powerful as information processed at conscious levels, and often more so. While a client is in hypnosis, his or her conscious mind will inevitably wander about from thought to thought; for those periods of time, which can be long or short, the client's unconscious mind can continue to take in the clinician's suggestions, and is still quite capable of responding to them meaningfully (Cheek, 1994; Crawford, 1990; Dixon, Brunet & Laurence, 1990).

The unconscious mind can process information at a more symbolic, metaphorical level than the conscious mind. While the conscious mind is occupied with rationally analyzing the words and noticing their effects, it is the unconscious that is more concerned with subjective meanings. This is the basis for the multiple level nature of hypnotic communication—that is, using wording and phrasing of suggestions to appeal at one level to the client's conscious mind by matching its understanding and associations of things, while simultaneously providing possibilities of new understandings to the unconscious mind (Hilgard, 1992; Woody, Bowers & Oakman, 1992).

IN DEFENSE OF THE MIND

The fact that information can be and often is processed without conscious awareness is a major factor in the fear some have that destructive or harmful information from the hypnotist is going to get in at an unconscious level and wreak havoc in the individual. Many people have not yet developed an appreciation of the mind's ability to protect itself. Every student of psychology, as well as anyone who has spent some time in the company of other people, learns about the classic defense mechanisms people employ to ward off threats from entering consciousness.

The defenses are unconscious, and are rooted in the person's need for self-esteem and the desire to avoid internal conflict if at all possible. These defenses are certainly relevant to hypnosis, and can demonstrate my point about the relative ability for self-defense (Fromm, 1992; Watkins, 1992).

THE DUALITY OF THE MIND

Characterizing the dual nature of mental functioning as "conscious" and "unconscious" has been abandoned by many in recent years in favor of characterizing mental functions by brain hemisphere. The two major hemispheres of the brain naturally have many common functions, but they are popularly characterized by their differences.

The left hemisphere of the brain corresponds roughly to the conscious mind. The left hemisphere, sometimes called the "verbal hemisphere," is responsible for the majority of speech functions. It is also often called the "logical hemisphere" because it is thought to contain the reasoning, analytical, and intellectual functions. Its focus on detail makes it more likely to "see the trees and not the forest," metaphorically speaking

The right hemisphere of the brain corresponds roughly to the unconscious. The right hemisphere is often called the "silent hemisphere" or the "intuitive hemisphere." It is said to contain a person's intuition and creativity, and is thought to operate on more symbolic and holistic levels than the left brain. Thus, the appreciation of and ability to create art and music are considered right brain functions. The right brain is said to contain the person's worldview and self-image, and is more likely to get the overview of things—"seeing the forest and not the trees," metaphorically speaking (Brown, 1991; Gabel, 1988).

The process of hypnosis in this "left brain–right brain" scheme of things is characterized as distracting and occupying the left hemisphere of the client while utilizing the resources of his or her right hemisphere. Language that is sensory-based, descriptive, and emotional, is more appealing to the right brain, and is the basis for Paul Watzlawick calling such language *The Language of Change* (1978).

Except under extreme conditions, the mind has the ability to protect itself from threats, sensory overload, and sensory isolation. The unconscious mind is not a significant danger to the person; rather it has the potential, if used therapeutically, to be a safe haven for one's inner self. For example, while one gets lost in thought while driving, a common experience, one's unconscious mind still operates the vehicle safely; the conscious mind pays attention only when some unusual situation arises that requires its attention. In defense of the mind is the mind (Gazzaniga, 1985; Hilgard, 1992).

CONCLUSION

However you conceptualize the mind, there is clearly a multiplicity present, with each component having some unique characteristics and with each offering its own contributions to subjective experience. Hypnosis as a tool is extremely useful in its ability to utilize more of the client's mental resources than other approaches typically do. Due to the enormous complexity of the human mind, and because of the uniqueness of each human being, respect for the personal power and integrity of each person is not just desirable, but mandatory.

REFERENCES

Brown, P. (1991). *The hypnotic brain.* New Haven, CT: Yale University Press.

Cheek, D. (1994). *Hypnosis: The application of ideomotor techniques.* Boston, MA: Allyn & Bacon.

Crawford, H. (1990). Cognitive and psychophysiological correlates of hypnotic responsiveness and hypnosis. In M. Fass & D. Brown (Eds.), *Creative mastery in hypnosis and hypnoanalysis: A festschift for Erika Fromm* (pp. 47–54). Hillsdale, NJ: Erlbaum.

Dixon, M., Brunet, A. & Laurence, J-R. (1990). Hypnotizability and automaticity: Toward a parallel distributed processing model of hypnotic responding. *Journal of Abnormal Psychology, 99,* 336–343.

Dixon, M. & Laurence, J-R. (1992). Two hundred years of hypnosis research: Questions resolved? Questions unanswered! In E. Fromm & M. Nash (Eds.), *Contemporary hypnosis research* (pp. 34–66). New York: Guilford.

Fromm, E. (1992). An ego-psychological theory of hypnosis. In E. Fromm & M. Nash (Eds.), *Contemporary hypnosis research* (pp. 131–148). New York: Guilford.

Gabel, S. (1988). The right hemisphere in imagery hypnosis, rapid eye movement sleep and dreaming: Empirical studies and tentative conclusions. *Journal of Nervous and Mental Disease, 176,* 323–331.

Gazzaniga, M. (1985). *The social brain: Discovering the networks of the mind.* New York: Basic Books.

Hilgard, E. (1986). *Divided consciousness: Multiple controls in human thought and action* (Rev. ed.). New York: John Wiley & Sons.

Hilgard, E. (1992). Dissociation and theories of hypnosis. In E. Fromm & M. Nash (Eds.), *Contemporary hypnosis research* (pp. 69–101). New York: Guilford.

Kihlstrom, J. (1984). Conscious, subconscious, unconscious: A cognitive perspective. In K. Bowers & D. Merchenbaum (Eds.), *The unconscious reconsidered* (pp.

149–211). New York: John Wiley & Sons.

Kihlstrom, J. (1987). The cognitive unconscious. *Science, 237*, 1445–1452.

McConkey, K. (1991). The construction and resolution of experience and behavior in hypnosis. In S. Lynn & J. Rhue (Eds.), *Theories of hypnosis: Current models and perspectives* (pp. 542–563). New York: Guilford.

Ornstein, R. (1986). *Multimind.* Boston: Houghton Mifflin.

Ornstein, R. (1991). *The evolution of consciousness.* New York: Prentice Hall.

Watkins, J. (1992). *Hypnoanalytic techniques: Clinical hypnosis* (Vol. 2). New York: Irvington.

Watzlawick, P. (1978). *The language of change.* New York: Basic Books.

Woody, E., Bowers, K. & Oakman, J. (1992). A conceptual analysis of hypnotic responsiveness: Experience, individual differences and context. In E. Fromm & M. Nash (Eds.), *Contemporary hypnosis research* (pp. 3–33). New York: Guilford.

Zeig, J. (Ed.) (1980). *A teaching seminar with Milton H. Erickson, M.D.* New York: Brunner/Mazel.

9

SUSCEPTIBILITY TO HYPNOSIS

The issue of who can be hypnotized (and who cannot) is one of the most controversial issues in the entire field of hypnosis. It has been researched and written about in numerous publications, both scientific and otherwise, by some of the most respected people in the field. Such research has typically described personality types and other characteristics (e.g., intelligence) of subjects that predispose them to favorable or unfavorable responses to hypnotic procedures. Many studies have also published statistical breakdowns of the general population into percentages of people who can be hypnotized to various depths of hypnosis as well as those few who apparently cannot be hypnotized at all.

The susceptibility issue was touched on briefly in the earlier chapter dealing with misconceptions about hypnosis, specifically in the discussion of the misconception that "only certain kinds of people can be hypnotized." This chapter expands on that discussion of susceptibility in order to allow you a greater degree of certainty in your work that the client you are working with can indeed experience hypnosis meaningfully.

TRADITIONAL VIEWS ON SUSCEPTIBILITY

Many researchers consider susceptibility to hypnosis as a personality trait comparable to other personality traits. In this view, it is unclear whether one is born with a high, medium, low, or absent "hypnotic susceptibility" biological structure, or whether this trait is acquired as a learned phenomenon through the socialization process. Regardless, in this view the presence or absence of the hypnotizability trait is a condition that remains relatively stable over time. In other words, if a

49

person lacks responsiveness to formal hypnosis induction procedures, that person is deemed a poor subject who is apparently unable to respond adequately to hypnosis. Further research studies on the reliability of this conclusion support it: Poor subjects tend to remain poor over time (in repeated attempts to induce hypnosis in the same person with the same or similar procedures) and good subjects tend to remain good over time (Banyai, 1991; Morgan, Johnson & Hilgard, 1974; Piccione, Hilgard & Zimbardo, 1989).

Elsewhere in the traditional literature on hypnosis, you can find discussion of other dimensions of hypnotic susceptibility that are more descriptive than mere statistical averages of responsiveness to standardized procedures. Such dimensions include age, intelligence, mental status, self-esteem, degree of fantasy proneness and imaginative skill, and relationship factors between clinician and client. Each dimension will be discussed from both a traditional and utilization perspective.

AGE AND HYPNOTIZABILITY

Much of the traditional literature promotes the idea that children, especially around the ages of seven to nine, are the best hypnotic subjects because of their active imaginations and willingness to follow directions. Other literature contradicts this, claiming that children's lesser ability to concentrate and their smaller reservoir of personal resources lead them to be poorer subjects.

One of the most common reasons why some practitioners come to doubt the responsiveness of children to hypnosis arises from the active nature of many children. As will be discussed later, adults generally inhibit voluntary activity when in hypnosis, but children often fidget and appear restless even though they may be very involved with the clinician and what he or she is doing. If you have a rigid expectation of how a client in hypnosis must look and behave, a fidgety child may be viewed as unaffected by hypnotic procedures.

Demanding inactivity (called "catalepsy") as evidence of hypnosis is an imposition on the child with an active nature, and simply is not necessary for your communications to have a meaningful effect. Children can be and often are highly responsive to appropriate interventions (Kohen & Olness, 1993; Olness & Gardner, 1988).

In general, age is a relatively minor consideration in assessing capacity for hypnosis. Age *is* a factor in determining the best methods for induction and utilization because of the need to use procedures that are appropriate to the age and background of the client, regardless of his or her age (Morgan & Hilgard, 1973).

INTELLIGENCE AND HYPNOTIZABILITY

Studies on hypnotic susceptibility have often suggested that the more intelligent the person, the better the hypnotic subject he or she will be. Such studies have been remarkably ambiguous in their findings. If there is a relationship between intelligence and hypnotizability, it is believed to be because of the positive relationship between intelligence and ability to concentrate (Spiegel & Spiegel, 1987; Weitzenhoffer, 1989).

Approaches should be molded to the capacity of the individual. Formulating goals and approaches that are consistent with the person's abilities is more the challenge in such special cases than is inducing hypnosis.

MENTAL STATUS AND HYPNOTIZABILITY

Much of the older literature that promotes the idea of psychotics' inability to be hypnotized will give the reason for their lack of responsiveness as an inability to concentrate. It is claimed they are unable to attend to the hypnotist's guidance due to their hallucinations, delusions, confusion, and inability to establish rapport. To a significant extent, this is true. However, individualized techniques that allow for the building of trust (rapport), that don't make too many demands too soon, and that are indirect enough to not arouse fear and suspicion can get in and work.

Of course, the degree of psychosis is a variable to consider—I doubt a manic-depressive in peak manic phase, for example, can be affected by a good hypnotist or anyone else. Likewise, cause of the psychosis is a noteworthy factor as well. For example, drug-induced psychosis is difficult to overcome. Persons with organically induced psychosis such as that associated with aging can respond to some hypnotic techniques successfully. Many older patients suffering senility whom I have worked with could not remember what they were doing five minutes before, but can remember with remarkable clarity things that occurred 50 years ago. Regressive techniques to early experiences can have a calming, soothing effect. Likewise, basic care of these and other psychotic patients, such as the care given during bathing and dressing, can have very positive effects (Murray-Jobsis, 1993; Spiegel, Detrick & Frischolz, 1982; Zindel, 1992).

SELF-ESTEEM AND HYPNOTIZABILITY

The self-esteem of the client is a major variable in his or her ability to respond meaningfully to the clinician's communications. It is your self-esteem that, in part, determines what you view as possible for yourself.

Self-esteem appears to be an entirely learned phenomenon, not a trait present at birth. Your experiences and, more importantly, the conclusions you draw from those experiences determine what you will view yourself as being capable of. Confronting a client's self-image directly in the form of contradicting it is rarely a successful maneuver in trying to change it. Typically, the client just gets the feeling the clinician really doesn't understand him or her.

A goal of using hypnosis is to enhance people's self-esteem. What is self-esteem? Certainly, there is no commonly accepted definition, but it clearly involves having an awareness for, acceptance of, and appreciation for, each of the aspects of self.

FANTASY PRONENESS, IMAGINATION AND HYPNOSIS

People vary in their styles and abilities to process information; some people are quite concrete and require highly detailed descriptions of experience they have already had in order to experience hypnosis, while others are capable of high level abstraction in which imagination and fantasy can run loose in their minds and generate meaningful experiences for them. How concrete or abstract one is in his or her thinking is a factor in responsiveness to hypnosis because of the subjective nature of the experience.

Every person has an imagination and an ability to fantasize, but some more so than others. Some people's imaginative powers are very concrete, others' are more abstract. This is one more variable to consider in formulating one's approach (Hilgard, 1970, 1974; Lynn & Nash, 1994; Lynn & Rhue, 1991).

RELATIONSHIP FACTORS AND HYPNOTIZABILITY

Rapport between clinician and client has always been considered a major factor in the therapeutic process, and rightly so. Rapport is, by my definition, a positive interrelationship between individuals based on understanding and trust. You have rapport when your client feels understood, and when he or she feels you have an appreciation for the value and complexity of his or her personal experience (Barber, 1991; Zeig & Rennick, 1991).

In the older methods of hypnosis, rapport was largely evidenced by the client's compliance with the hypnotist's authority. This kind of one-sided relationship may still be considered by some to be a viable choice for the hypnotic interaction. However, the more balanced type of cooperative relationship inherent in the utilization approach is generally a more respectful and collaborative relationship. Hypnosis can be viewed as a naturally arising response within a special kind of relationship, one of mutual responsibility and accountability. The clinician's leads are determined by the client's leads, and vice versa. Hypnosis is a continuous process of adjusting and readjusting to each other, even though at any given moment one or the other might seem to be setting the pace of the interaction. A continuous feedback loop is essential in this approach, with feedback from the client determining the clinician's leads, and feedback from the clinician determining the client's leads. This kind of relationship is one that differs appreciably from those perspectives of the hypnotic relationship in which the client is supposed to obediently follow the leads of the clinician, and where failure to do so signals "resistance." Responsiveness to the client allows a clinician to offer suggestions both in a form and at a pace that maximize the client's ability to respond (Gfeller, 1993; Gfeller, Lynn & Pribble, 1987; Gilligan, 1987; Zeig, 1980).

HYPNOTIC SUSCEPTIBILITY TESTS

There are a number of established hypnotic susceptibility scales available for use should you desire to formally test the responsiveness of a client. Most of these scales attempt to standardize hypnotic behavior by first inducing hypnosis in a person, and then giving him or her tests in order to determine the degree of depth and responsiveness. In such tests, the client must pass and fail the various tests, and the administrator of the susceptibility scale records the test results in order to establish a profile of the person's hypnotic capacities.

The following tests, arranged in alphabetical order, have been used to assess various aspects of an individual's hypnotic responsiveness:

Barber Suggestibility Scale (Barber, 1976).

Carleton University Responsivenss to Suggestions Scale (Spanos, Radtke, Hodgins, Stram & Bertrand, 1983).

Creative Imagination Scale (Wilson & Barber, 1977).

Davis-Husband Scale (Davis & Husband, 1931).

Field Inventory (Self-report) (Field, 1965).

Friedlander-Sarbin Scale of Hypnotic Depth (Friedlander & Sarbin, 1938).

Harvard Group Scale of Hypnotic Susceptibility (Shor & Orne, 1962).

Hypnotic Experience Questionnaire - Short form (Matheson, Shu & Bart, 1989).

Hypnotic Induction Profile (Spiegel, 1972; Stern, Spiegel & Nee, 1979).

LeCron-Bordeaux Scale (LeCron & Bordeaux, 1947).

Phenomenology of Consciousness Inventory (Self-report) (Pekala, 1982).

Self-Report Scales of Hypnotic Depth (Self-report) (Tart, 1970).

Stanford Hypnotic Clinical Scale (Morgan & Hilgard, 1979).

Stanford Hypnotic Susceptibility Scale, Forms A & B (Weitzenhoffer & Hilgard, 1959).

Stanford Hypnotic Susceptibility Scale, Form C (Weitzenhoffer & Hilgard, 1962).

Stanford Profile Scales of Hypnotic Susceptibility, Forms I & II (Weitzenhoffer & Hilgard, 1963).

Tellegen Absorption Scale (Tellegen & Atkinson, 1974).

The debate continues over just how useful clinical scales are in treatment. Their value in research is beyond question. However, it is unclear how relevant a response to a standardized, therefore nonindividualized, test item is to eventual clinical results obtained.

REFERENCES

Banyai, E. (1991). Toward a social-psychobiological model of hypnosis. In S. Lynn & J. Rhue (Eds.), *Theories of hypnosis: Current models and perspectives* (pp. 564–598). New York: Guilford.

Barber, J. (1965). Measuring "hypnotic-like" suggestibility without "hypnotic induction": Psychometric properties, norms, and variables influencing response to the Barber Suggestibility Scale (BSS). *Psychological Reports, 16*, 806–844.

Barber, J. (1991). The locksmith model: Accessing hypnotic responsiveness. In S. Lynn & J. Rhue (Eds.), *Theories of hypnosis: Current models and perspectives* (pp. 241–274). New York: Guilford.

Barber, T. (1976). *Hypnosis.* New York: Pergamon.

Davis, L. & Husband, R. (1931). A study of hypnotic susceptibility in relation to personality traits. *Journal of Abnormal and Social Psychology, 26*, 175–182.

Field, P. (1965). An inventory scale of hypnotic depth. *International Journal of Clinical and Experimental Hypnosis, 13*, 238–249.

Frederick, C. & McNeal, S. (1993). From strength to strength: "Inner strength" with immature ego states. *American Journal of Clinical Hypnosis, 35*, 4, 250–256.

Friedlander, J. & Sarbin, T. (1938). The depth of hypnosis. *Journal of Abnormal and Social Psychology, 33*, 453–475.

Gfeller, J. (1993). Enhancing hypnotizability and treatment responsiveness. In J. Rhue, S. Lynn & I. Kirsch (Eds.), *Handbook of clinical hypnosis* (pp. 235–250).

Washington, DC: American Psychological Association.

Gfeller, J., Lynn, S. & Pribble, W. (1987). Enhancing hypnotic susceptibility: Interpersonal and rapport factors. *Journal of Personality and Social Psychology, 52*, 586–595.

Gilligan, S. (1987). *Therapeutic trances: The cooperation principle in Ericksonian hypnotherapy.* New York: Brunner/Mazel.

Hammond, D. (Ed.) (1990). *Handbook of hypnotic suggestions and metaphors.* New York: Norton.

Hilgard, J. (1970). *Personality and hypnosis: A study of imaginative involvement.* Chicago: University of Chicago Press.

Hilgard, J. (1974). Imaginative involvement: Some characteristics of the highly hypnotizable and non-hypnotizable. *International Journal of Clinical and Experimental Hypnosis, 22*, 138–156.

Kohen, D. & Olness, K. (1993). Hypnotherapy with children. In J. Rhue, S. Lynn & I. Kirsch (Eds.), *Handbook of clinical hypnosis* (pp. 257–381). Washington, DC: American Psychological Association.

LeCron, L. & Bordeaux, J. (1947). *Hypnotism today.* New York: Grune & Stratton.

Lynn, S. & Nash, M. (1994). Truth in memory: Ramifications for psychotherapy and hypnotherapy. *American Journal of Clinical Hypnosis, 36*, 3, 194–208.

Lynn, S. & Rhue, J. (1991). An integrative model of hypnosis. In S. Lynn & J. Rhue (Eds.), *Theories of hypnosis: Current models and perspectives* (pp. 397–438). New York: Guilford.

Matheson, G., Shu, K. & Bart, C. (1989). A validation study of a Short-Form Hypnotic-Experience Questionnaire and its relationship to hypnotizability. *American Journal of Clinical Hypnosis, 32*, 1, 17–26.

McNeal, S. & Frederick, C. (1993). Inner strength and other techniques for ego strengthening. *American Journal of Clinical Hypnosis, 35*, 3, 170–178.

Morgan, A. & Hilgard, E. (1973). Age differences in susceptibility to hypnosis. *International Journal of Clinical and Experimental Hypnosis, 21*, 75–85.

Morgan, A. & Hilgard, J. (1979). The Stanford hypnotic clinical scale for adults. *American Journal of Clinical Hypnosis, 21*, 134–147.

Morgan, A., Johnson, D. & Hilgard, E. (1974). The stability of hypnotic susceptibility: A longitudinal study. *International Journal of Clinical and Experimental Hypnosis, 22*, 249–257.

Murray-Jobsis, J. (1993). The borderline patient and the psychotic patient. In J. Rhue, S. Lynn & I. Kirsch (Eds.), *Handbook of clinical hypnosis* (pp. 425–451). Washington, DC: American Psychological Association.

Olness, K. & Gardner, G. (1988). *Hypnosis and hypnotherapy with children* (2nd. ed.). New York: Grune & Stratton.

Pekala, R. (1982). *The phenomenology of consciousness inventory.* Thorndale, PA: Psychophenomenological Concepts.

Phillips, M. & Frederick, C. (1992). The use of hypnotic age progression as prognostic, ego-strengthening, and integrating techniques. *American Journal of Clinical Hypnosis, 35*, 2, 99–108.

Piccione, C., Hilgard, E. & Zimbardo, P. (1989). On the stability of measured hypnotizability over a 25-year period. *Journal of Personality and Social Psychology, 56*, 289–295.

Shor, R. & Orne, E. (1962). *The Harvard Group Scale of Hypnotic Susceptibility.* Palo Alto, CA: Consulting Psychological Press.

Spanos, N., Radtke, H., Hodgins, D. Stram, H., & Bertrand, L. (1983). The Carleton University Responsiveness to Suggestion Scale: Normative data and psychometric properties. *Psychological Reports, 53,* 523–535.

Spiegel, D., Detrick, D. & Frischolz, E. (1982). Hypnotizability and psychopathology. *American Journal of Psychiatry, 139,* 431–437.

Spiegel, H. (1972). An eye-roll test for hypnotizability. *American Journal of Clinical Hypnosis, 15,* 25–28.

Spiegel, H. & Spiegel, D. (1987). *Trance and treatment: Clinical uses of hypnosis.* Washington, DC: American Psychiatric Press.

Stanton, H. (1989). Ego-enhancement: A five-step approach. *American Journal of Clinical Hypnosis, 31,* 3, 192–198.

Stern, D., Spiegel, H. & Nee, J. (1979). The hypnotic induction profile: Normative observations, reliability, and validity. *American Journal of Clinical Hypnosis, 31,* 109–132.

Tart, C. (1970). Self-Report Scales of Hypnotic Depth. *International Journal of Clinical and Experimental Hypnosis, 18,* 105–125.

Tellegen, A. & Atkinson, G. (1974). Openness to absorbing and self-altering experiences ("absorption"), a trait related to hypnotic susceptibility. *Journal of Abnormal Psychology, 83,* 268–277.

Weitzenhoffer, A. & Hilgard, E. (1959). *The Stanford scale of hypnotic susceptibility, forms A and B.* Palo Alto, CA: Consulting Psychologists Press.

Weitzenhoffer, A. & Hilgard, E. (1962). *The Stanford scale of hypnotic susceptibility, form C.* Palo Alto, CA: Consulting Psychologists Press.

Weitzenhoffer, A. & Hilgard, E. (1963). *The Stanford profile scales of hypnotic susceptibility, I and II.* Palo Alto, CA: Consulting Psychologists Press.

Weitzenhoffer, A. (1989). *The practice of hypnotism* (Vol.1). New York: John Wiley & Sons.

Wilson, S. & Barber, T. (1977). *The Creative Imagination Scale as a measure of hypnotic responsiveness: Applications to experimental and clinical hypnosis.* Medfield, MA: Medfield Foundation.

Zeig, J. (Ed.) (1980). *A teaching seminar with Milton H. Erickson, M.D.* New York: Brunner/Mazel.

Zeig, J. & Rennick, P. (1991). Ericksonian hypnotherapy: A communications approach to hypnosis. In S. Lynn & J. Rhue (Eds.), *Theories of hypnosis: Current models and perspectives.* (pp. 275–300). New York: Guilford.

Zindel, P. (1992). Hypnosis in psychotherapy of schizophrenic patients and borderline patients. In W. Bongartz (Ed.), *Hypnosis: 175 years after Mesmer: Recent developments in theory and application* (pp. 309–313). Konstanz, Germany: Universitats verlag Konstanz.

10

THE EXPERIENCE OF HYPNOSIS

Hypnosis is a highly subjective experience, for no two people experience it in exactly the same way. Presented in this chapter are some of the more prominent general characteristics, both psychological and physical, associated with the hypnotic experience. Table 1 lists common characteristics manifested by the individual in hypnosis.

These characteristics necessitate communicating differently to a person in hypnosis than you might in more routine interactions.

PSYCHOLOGICAL CHARACTERISTICS OF THE HYPNOTIC STATE

Selective Attention

If you have ever heard or used the phrase, "He only sees what he wants to see," then you have an awareness that human beings can notice what they choose to notice. By implication, people can also *not* notice what they choose not to. This phenomenon is referred to as "selective attention," the ability to deliberately focus on one portion of an experience while "tuning out" the rest.

The process of selective attention is an instrumental factor in the hypnotic interaction (Crawford & Gruzelier, 1992; Weitzenhoffer, 1989). The client must gradually selectively attend to the provided suggestions and narrow his or her attention to whatever internal associations the suggestions stimulate. The client's focus is generally inward, and so even though external events may be noticed and responded to, they actually account only for a small minority of the client's attention. The unconscious becomes prominent in its ability to respond to things outside of the person's conscious attentional field. I have just described a basis for the next characteristic I will discuss: Dissociation.

Table 1
The Experience of Hypnosis

Experiential and selective absorption of attention (Spiegel & Spiegel, 1987).

Effortless expression (Gilligan, 1987).

Experiential, nonconceptual involvement (Erickson, Rossi & Rossi, 1976).

Willingness to experiment (Gilligan, 1987).

Flexibility in time/space relations (Erickson, Rossi & Rossi, 1976).

Alterations of perception (Erickson & Rossi, 1979).

Fluctuations in degree of involvement (Gilligan, 1987).

Motoric/verbal inhibition (Erickson, Rossi & Rossi, 1976).

Trance logic; reduction in reality testing (Shor, 1959).

Symbolic processing (Zeig, 1980).

Time distortion (Erickson, Rossi & Rossi, 1976).

Amnesia (full or partial) (Erickson, Rossi & Rossi, 1976; Rossi, 1993).

Dissociation

While the person in hypnosis has his or her attention selectively focused on the suggestions of the clinician and whatever unconscious associations may be triggered as a result, there is a division occurring between the conscious and unconscious minds. The conscious mind is occupied with the hypnotic procedures, while the unconscious is actively searching for symbolic meanings, past associations, and appropriate responses. This separation of conscious and unconscious dimensions of functioning during the hypnotic experience is accomplished in varying degrees with different people, and is called "dissociation." The fact that the conscious and unconscious minds can be divided to some extent and utilized as interdependent yet independent entities is the backbone of hypnosis. Facilitating dissociation through your hypnotic approaches allows you to have more direct access to the client's unconscious mind's many resources and deeper knowledge of the inner workings of the individual.

Another way of considering the dissociative nature of the hypnotic experience is through the "parallel awareness" which is amplified during hypnosis. The client in hypnosis has multiple awarenesses, each operating on a separate level. One of these levels is a relatively objective one that has a realistic understanding of the nature of the experience, a part of the person Ernest Hilgard (1986) called the "hidden observer." The "hidden observer" is separated (dissociated) from the immediacy of the suggested experiences, and can maintain a degree of objectivity about the experience. This dissociative characteristic of the hypnotic state allows the client to attend to and respond to suggestions while at the same time observing himself or herself go through the experience (Hilgard, 1992; Kirsch & Council, 1992; McConkey, 1986).

Increased Responsiveness to Suggestion

The attentional and dissociational factors described above typically lead to an increased responsiveness to suggestion. The hypnotic inter- action has been defined as a therapeutic and/or educational one for the client, and the capacity for influence is certainly present. The client selectively attends to the suggestions of the clinician, and the sugges- tions trigger responses and associations within him or her. Increased responsiveness is evidenced as a greater willingness in the client to be guided by the suggestions of the clinician, most probably because of the expectation that there is something to be gained by accepting them.

Responsiveness, therefore, is not to be confused with gullibility, or noncritical acceptance. The hypnotic state actually *amplifies* a person's range of choices, including the choice to to reject a suggestion that isn't particularly well fitting (Hilgard, 1965; Kirsch, Lynn & Rhue, 1993). The increased responsiveness to suggestion is a choice on the part of the client to be guided by someone he or she trusts and feels is wanting to help. If the personal, interpersonal, and contextual dynamics are not favorable, responsiveness is nonexistent. The result is what is classi- cally termed "resistance."

Subjective Interpretation

How a given person will respond to a word or phrase is unpredictable. Remember, the person is using his or her own frame of reference (i.e., experiences, understanding) to make meaning out of your words. The best you can do is use words carefully enough to leave as little room as possible (or as much room, as the case may be) for misinterpretation. Training in hypnosis with peers allows for the kind of honest feedback on the impact of your words and phrases that your clients are highly unlikely to provide. Finding out which of your communications facili- tated the hypnotic experience and which hindered it are two of the most valuable aspects of small-group training in clinical hypnotherapy (Erickson & Rossi, 1979, 1981; Matthews, Lankton & Lankton, 1993).

"Trance Logic"

A characteristic of the hypnotic state that is eminently practical in its clinical applications is called "trance logic." This refers to the client's lack of need for his or her experience to be entirely realistic or rational. In other words, the client can, at least temporarily, accept the suggested reality, however illogical and objectively impossible it may be, as if it were the only reality.

Trance logic is a voluntary state of acceptance of suggestions on the part of the client without the critical evaluation taking place that would, of course, destroy the validity or meaningfulness of some suggestions. The opportunity for the client to respond "as if" something were real can be a gateway to deeper feelings and issues appropriate for therapeutic interventions (Lynn & Rhue, 1991; Orne, 1959; Sheehan & McConkey, 1982).

Relaxation

You can be in hypnosis without necessarily being relaxed, but the relaxation of mind and body is a general characteristic most people associate with hypnosis. Most hypnotic processes do involve relaxation as a way of facilitating the dissociation of the conscious from the unconscious mind. Relaxation feels good to clients, alters their experience of themselves in a clear-cut way, and may even convince them that they have, in fact, been hypnotized (Benson & Carol, 1974; Edmonston, 1991; Mitchell & Lundy, 1986).

The relaxation associated with hypnosis surfaces in a number of physical changes (described in the next section) and in a voluntary passivity in which the client experiences doing almost anything as taking too much effort. Asking the client to talk, move, or think is often met with apparent inaction on the part of the client, simply because what has been suggested requires more energy than he or she cares to expend! This is another reason to take a more easygoing approach rather than a demanding one, as it can allow the client to experience hypnosis in his or her own way without having to "perform."

PHYSICAL CHARACTERISTICS OF THE HYPNOTIC STATE

How do you know your client is in hypnosis? The answer is a definite... you don't. At precisely what moment a person has gone from his or her usual state of awareness to a more focused state of hypnosis is unknown. Given that the hypnotic state is a state differing from everyday mental experience only by degrees and not kind, there are no clear boundaries that separate one's "usual" state from the hypnotic state. Likewise, there are no clear dividing lines between the various degrees of hypnotic depth. With experience, however, you will likely notice a variety of physical characteristics associated with hypnosis that may be used as general indicators of its presence (Erickson, Rossi & Rossi, 1976).

Physical indicators that may be useful to observe include:

1. Muscular relaxation—Notice the person's level of tension carried in the body and especially the facial muscles both before and during your work for comparison.
2. Muscular twitching—As the body and mind relax, often there are spasms that are wholly involuntary and are related to the neurological changes that take place with relaxation.
3. Lachrymation—As the person relaxes, occasionally the eyes may tear. Some automatically assume the person is upset and shedding a tear, but that is an unjustifiable leap to a possibly erroneous conclusion. If in doubt, ask!
4. Eye closure with fluttering eyelids—As the person begins to shift his or her focus and enter hypnosis, the eyelids may flutter at a very fast rate and usually outside of awareness. Also, rapid eye movements under the eyelid are observable throughout much of the hypnotic process, even more so if your methods involve a lot of visualization.
5. Change in breathing rate—A change, either speeding up or slowing down, of breathing is typical. Observe the client's breathing patterns before and during the process for comparison. Some people's breathing becomes shallower, some deeper; some breathe from the chest, others from the diaphragm.
6. Change in pulse rate—A change, either speeding up but usually slowing down, of the pulse is also typical. When the client is sitting back, you can usually observe the pulsing of the carotid artery in his or her neck. Or if you prefer (and you have the client's permission) you can hold the client's wrist "to be supportive" and take a reading of his or her radial pulse.
7. Jaw relaxes—Often the person's lower jaw drops and seems subjectively to weigh so much that it takes conscious effort to close it. (I've known people who wouldn't participate in group hypnosis because of their embarrassing tendency to drool!)
8. Catalepsy—An inhibition of voluntary motion that is uniquely reflective of the absorption of hypnosis. Unlike sleep, in which you are in almost constant motion, the person in hypnosis makes very

few, if any, movements. It simply takes too much effort. Often, the client feels dissociated from his or her body anyway, and so forgets about it.

Every once in a while, and this is especially true of children, you may experience someone who moves around a lot. In one training course, I had a student the class nicknamed "The Thrasher." When he experienced hypnosis, he liked to roll on the floor and wiggle around quite a bit. On disengaging, he described how good it felt to relax his body through movement. Even though movement may seem excessive or disruptive to you, your client may still be in hypnosis.

Each of the physical characteristics described above may be used as general indicators of hypnosis, but no one sign alone can tell you what your client is actually experiencing internally. In a sense, the clinician is a visitor to someone else's world, and so should be observant, cautious, and, above all, respectful. Much of your assessment of when to shift from one phase of your hypnosis session to another, e.g., going from induction into utilization, will be based on how well you observe changes in your client's body and demeanor. Taking a baseline reading of his or her muscular tension, breathing and pulse rates, and anything else you can find before beginning can give you the opportunity to notice changes taking place as you continue which suggest the development of a state different from the client's original one. You really can't always know what the content of the person's experience is, but you can observe changes that suggest some impact from your guidance. The more skilled you become in observing such changes, the more comfortable you can be in adapting your suggestions spontaneously to the ongoing experience of the client (Grinder & Bandler, 1981; O'Hanlon, 1987).

REFERENCES

Benson, H. & Carol, M. (1974). The relaxation response. *Psychiatry, 37*, 37–46.

Crawford, H. & Gruzelier, J. (1992). A midstream view of the neuropsychophysiology of hypnosis: Recent research and future directions. In E. Fromm & M. Nash (Eds.), *Contemporary hypnosis research* (pp. 227–266). New York: Guilford.

Edmonston, W. (1991). Anesis. In S. Lynn & J. Rhue (Eds.), *Theories of hypnosis: Current models and perspectives* (pp. 197–237). New York: Guilford.

Erickson, M., Rossi, E. & Rossi, S. (1976). *Hypnotic realities: The induction of clinical hypnosis and forms of indirect suggestion.* New York: Irvington.

Erickson, M. & Rossi, E. (1979). *Hypnotherapy: An exploratory casebook.* New York: Irvington.

Erickson, M. & Rossi, E. (1981). *Experiencing hypnosis: Therapeutic approaches to altered states.* New York: Irvington.

Gilligan, S. (1987). *Therapeutic trances: The cooperation principle in Ericksonian hypnotherapy.* New York: Brunner/Mazel.

Grinder, J. and Bandler, R. (1981). *Trance-formations: Neuro-Linguistic Programming and the structure of hypnosis.* Moab, UT: Real People Press.

Hilgard, E. (1965). *Hypnotic susceptibility.* New York: Harcourt, Brace & World.

Hilgard, E. (1986). *Divided consciousness: Multiple controls in human thought and action* (Rev. ed.). New York: John Wiley & Sons.

Hilgard, E. (1992). Dissociation and theories of hypnosis. In E. Fromm & M. Nash (Eds.), *Contemporary hypnosis research* (pp. 69–101). New York: Guilford.

Kirsch, I. & Council, J. (1992). Situational and personality correlates of hypnotic responsiveness. In E. Fromm & M. Nash (Eds.), *Contemporary hypnosis research* (pp. 267–291). New York: Guilford.

Kirsch, I., Lynn, S. & Rhue, J. (1993). Introduction to clinical hypnosis. In J. Rhue, S. Lynn & I. Kirsch (Eds.), *Handbook of clinical hypnosis* (pp. 3–22). Washington, DC: American Psychological Association.

Lynn, S. & Rhue, J. (1991). An integrative model of hypnosis. In S. Lynn & J. Rhue (Eds.), *Theories of hypnosis: Current models and perspectives* (pp. 397–438). New York: Guilford.

Matthews, W., Lankton, S. & Lankton, C. (1993). An Ericksonian model of hypnotherapy. In J. Rhue, S. Lynn & I. Kirsch (Eds.), *Handbook of clinical hypnosis* (pp. 187–214). Washington, DC: American Psychiatric Press.

McConkey, K. (1986). Opinions about hypnosis and self-hypnosis before and after hypnotic testing. *International Journal of Clinical and Experimental Hypnosis, 34,* 311–319.

Mitchell, G. & Lundy, R. (1986). The effects of relaxation and imagery inductions on responses to suggestions. *International Journal of Clinical and Experimental Hypnosis, 34,* 98–109.

O'Hanlon, W. (1987). *Taproots: Underlying principles of Milton Erickson's therapy and hypnosis.* New York: Norton.

Orne, M. (1959). The nature of hypnosis: Artifact and essence. *Journal of Abnormal and Social Psychology, 58,* 277–299.

Rossi, E. (1993). *The psychobiology of mind-body healing* (Rev. ed.). New York: Norton.

Sheehan, P. & McConkey, K. (1982). *Hypnosis and experience: The exploration of phenomena and process.* Hillsdale, NJ: Erlbaum.

Shor, R. (1959). Hypnosis and the concept of the generalized reality-orientation. *American Journal of Psychotherapy, 13,* 582–602.

Spiegel, H. & Spiegel, D. (1987). *Trance and treatment: Clinical uses of hypnosis.* Washington, DC: American Psychiatric Press.

Weitzenhoffer, A. (1989). *The practice of hypnotism* (Vol. 1). New York: John Wiley & Sons.

Zeig, J. (Ed.) (1980). *A teaching seminar with Milton H. Erickson, M.D.* New York: Brunner/Mazel.

Zeig, J. & Rennick, P. (1991). Ericksonian hypnotherapy: A communications approach to hypnosis. In S. Lynn & J. Rhue (Eds.), *Theories of hypnosis: Current models and perspectives* (pp. 275–300). New York: Guilford.

11

CONDITIONS FOR DOING HYPNOSIS

In this chapter, I would like to explore some of the variables beyond your communication patterns and therapeutic relationship that can affect your work. These variables are characterized as "Environmental" and "Physical."

ENVIRONMENTAL VARIABLES

There are certain environmental conditions that I think are desirable for doing hypnosis, but they are not absolutely essential. First, working in a relatively quiet atmosphere is helpful. An atmosphere that is free of intruding or obnoxious noise is obviously less distracting to the client, allowing him or her to focus more on internal rather than on external experiences. Realistically, however, phones ring, doors get knocked on, people converse outside your door (if you even have a door), traffic zooms by, planes pass overhead, people drop heavy objects, people sneeze, pets knock over vases, kids argue.... In other words, no environment is perfectly quiet and free from external noise — nor does it have to be. The key to helping the client focus internally without being distracted by external events lies in your ability to *tie those events into the process* (Bandler & Grinder, 1979; Zeig, 1980, 1985).

Another environmental factor that may be helpful is the use of soft, soothing lighting. Soft lighting can help create a comfortable atmosphere, and facilitate comfort. I would not recommend lighting that is too dim, nor would I recommend darkness. Candlelight may be all right for some, too esoteric for others (like me).

A third environmental factor affecting the client's ability to relax is the furniture. Beds or couches to lie prone on may be too suggestive and furthermore are more likely to put the client to sleep. Furniture should be comfortable and support the client's head and body. As the client relaxes, his body tends to become heavy; aches of the neck and back can easily result if the client doesn't get adequate physical support. Recliner chairs are quite good for this reason (Alman & Lambrou, 1992; Weitzenhoffer, 1989).

Lighting, furniture, and environmental sound factors are less important factors than how you use them. The key point thus far is to *use whatever happens as a part of the process,* framing the intrusive event as being perfectly all right (Grinder & Bandler, 1981; Kelly, 1993; Stone, 1986).

PHYSICAL VARIABLES

Certain physical conditions are also worthy of consideration when one is doing hypnosis. I refer here not to physical health, but to transient physical experiences that may play a role in the hypnotic encounter. Physically, it helps if the client is comfortable, i.e., the body is adequately supported, clothing is not restrictive or binding, the temperature is comfortable, and mentally the client isn't feeling rushed or distracted by other things demanding immediate attention.

It is important that the client have nothing in his or her mouth (e.g., gum, candy) that could cause him or her to choke as he or she relaxes. Also, many people wear contact lenses, and some contact lenses are constructed in such a way that if the client closes his or her eyes even briefly (a few minutes), the lenses irritate the eyes to the point of becoming painful. Ask the client if he or she would like to remove glasses, contact lenses, shoes, or whatever else might inhibit his or her focus from going inward in a meaningful way.

Other physical considerations include drug or alcohol influences, which are typically counterproductive to doing effective work. Prescribed medications may be excepted, but even these may potentially hinder effective hypnotic responsiveness. Similar inhibitions can exist for the overtired or exhausted client who may be easy to put to sleep but is difficult to get to focus internally in a useful way (Beahrs, Carlin & Shehorn, 1974; Spiegel, 1986).

REFERENCES

Alman, B. & Lambrou, P. (1992). *Self-hypnosis: The complete manual for health and self-change.* New York: Brunner/Mazel.

Bandler, R. & Grinder, J. (1979). *Frogs into princes.* Moab, UT: Real People Press.

Beahrs, J., Carlin, A. & Shehorn, J. (1974). Impact of psychoactive drugs on hypnotizability. *American Journal of Clinical Hypnosis, 16*, 267–269.

Grinder, J. & Bandler, R. (1981). *Trance-formations: Neuro-Linguistic Programming and the structure of hypnosis.* Moab, UT: Real People Press.

Kelly, S. (1993). The use of music as a hypnotic suggestion. *American Journal of Clinical Hypnosis, 36*, 3, 83–90.

Spiegel, D. (1986). Effects of psychoactive medication on hypnosis. In B. Zilbergeld, M. Edelstein & D. Araoz (Eds.), *Hypnosis: Questions and answers* (pp. 345–349). New York: Norton.

Stone, J. (1986). Presentations of doctor and office to facilitate hypnosis. In B. Zilbergeld, M. Edelstein & D. Araoz (Eds.), *Hypnosis: Questions and answers* (pp. 69–75). New York: Norton.

Weitzenhoffer, A. (1989). *The practice of hypnotism* (Vol. 2). New York: John Wiley & Sons.

Zeig, J. (Ed.) (1980). *A teaching seminar with Milton H. Erickson, M.D.* New York: Brunner/Mazel.

Zeig, J. (1985). *Experiencing Erickson: An introduction to the man and his work.* New York: Brunner/Mazel.

Section II

PRACTICE

12

STRUCTURING SUGGESTIONS

The focus in this chapter is on some of the interpersonal communication variables of hypnotic patterns, specifically the communication styles and structures of hypnotic suggestions.

COMMUNICATION STYLES

Appreciating the differences both in the information processing styles and in the abilities of the conscious and unconscious minds is prerequisite to the effective use of hypnosis. Formulating suggestions that are more likely to appeal to the unconscious mind's worldview is one of the ways hypnosis derives its strength.

There are two major categories of hypnotic communications: direct and indirect. Not only are they *not* mutually exclusive, but I doubt it is possible (or desirable) to do an effective hypnotic process exclusively in one form or the other. Realistically, both styles will be evident in a given process at various times. Furthermore, each suggestion will vary in the degree of directness, as if on a continuum with "direct" at one pole and "indirect" at the other. The question of which style to use at a given moment depends on the nature of the suggestion (considering factors such as its potential for threatening the client) and the degree of responsiveness of the client (Alman & Carney, 1980; Erickson & Rossi, 1979; Zeig & Rennick, 1991).

Direct Suggestions

Direct suggestions are those that deal either with the problem at hand or the specific response desired overtly and clearly. They are not known

---

Table 2
Basic Hypnotic Suggestion Structures and Styles

Positive Suggestions

    "You can do X"

Negative Suggestions

    "You cannot do X"

Direct Suggestions

    "You can do X"

Indirect Suggestions

    "I knew someone who enjoyed doing X"

Process Suggestions

    "You can have a special memory"

Content Suggestions

    "You can remember your third grade teacher"

Permissive Styles

    "You can allow yourself to do X"

Authoritarian Styles

    "You will do X"

Posthypnotic Suggestions

    "Later, when you are in situation A, you can do X"

---

for their subtlety. Direct suggestions refer to the person's conscious experience a great deal, and they typically provide specific solutions to problems, along with detailed instructions about how to respond.

Commonly, to begin hypnosis, the clinician will want the client to close his or her eyes. If the clinician chooses a direct approach, he or she might offer any of the following direct suggestions:

Close your eyes.

Please close your eyes.

You can close your eyes.

Let your eyes close.

I would like you to close your eyes.

The advantages of direct suggestions include: 1) their direct relevance to the matters at hand (easing conscious worries in the client about your ability to deal directly with his or her concerns); 2) their ability to keep the client's goal well defined and in sight; 3) their direct involvement of the client in the process in an active way; and 4) their ability to serve as a model for the resolution of any future problems that arise through the direct development of a conscious problem-solving strategy.

The disadvantages of direct suggestions include their overreliance on a conscious willingness to follow suggestions, making less use of the resources of the unconscious mind. Also, direct suggestions are much more likely to engender resistance in the client by dealing so directly with his problems, potentially a threatening experience. Threatening the client increases the likelihood of defensive reactions, not the least of which is the rejection of suggestions.

Appreciating the advantages and disadvantages of the use of direct suggestions is necessary to allow you to make an informed decision as to when their use will most likely result in a successful hypnotic experience (Crasilneck & Hall, 1985; Kroger, 1977; Spiegel & Spiegel, 1987; Weitzenhoffer, 1989).

Indirect Suggestions

Indirect suggestions are those that relate to either the problem at hand or the specific desired response in a covert and, therefore, unobtrusive way. They can be quite subtle. Such suggestions do not usually relate directly to the person's conscious experience. Rather, they are indirectly related and thus require the client to interpret them in an idiosyncratic way in order to make meaning of them. Use of indirect suggestions can have the client wondering at a conscious level what you are talking about, while at the same time his or her unconscious mind is associating what you are saying to his or her internal experience (underlying dynamic processes), thus paving the way for change to take place.

Indirect suggestions can take numerous forms, including storytelling, analogies, jokes, puns, homework assignments, and disguised and embedded suggestions. Any communication device that causes or requires the client to respond without directly telling or asking him or her to do so involves indirect suggestion to some degree.

If you suspect, on the basis of feedback from your client, that you would be more likely to get eye closure through indirect methods, you might offer any of the following suggestions:

A good hypnotic subject begins by closing his or her eyes.

Can you allow your eyes to close?

Many of my clients like to sit in that chair with their eyes closed.

Isn't it nice not to have to listen with your eyes open?

I wonder what you will think of that will allow you to comfortably
  CLOSE YOUR EYES.

The advantages of the indirect approaches relate primarily to their
greater utilization of the unconscious mind's resources in the client's
own behalf. When suggestions are presented in the form of triggers for
old or new associations that may be therapeutic to experience, more of
the person is involved in the therapy at multiple levels. Furthermore, by
having a greater distance between the suggestion and its intended target
emotion or behavior, there is less need for resistant defenses. Such
distance may also create confusion in the client about how the suggestions relate to personal improvement, thus paving the way for the client
to interpret the suggestions in whatever way they will be useful to him
or her. By not forcing the client to respond to your arbitrary demands,
you demonstrate a greater respect for the client, which is a highly
desirable approach (Brown, 1991; Lankton & Lankton, 1983; Zeig, 1980).

The disadvantages of the indirect style include the client's possible
fear or anxiety that the clinician is unable or unwilling to deal directly
with the problem—"If the therapist can't, how can I?" The clinician may
then be viewed as evasive or incompetent, and the client may feel
manipulated and even cheated. Another disadvantage is that the client's
unconscious responses may allow for alleviation of the problem, but
may leave the client consciously wondering how the change occurred.
The problem may be solved, but the solution may not leave the client
with access to patterns for solving future problems (Lehrer, 1986; Yapko,
1983).

Choosing A Style

The guidelines for choosing a style and the degree to which that style
should be used are based on two major factors: the degree of insight
desirable or necessary to allow the intervention to work, and the degree
of responsiveness of the client.

Some clients demand understanding at a conscious level, asking
"Why?" a lot. Others are much more interested in getting some change
to occur in the problem, no matter what it takes. The more a person seeks
conscious understanding and tries to engage you on that level, the more
an indirect approach will disrupt his or her normal pattern, increasing
the likelihood of change. Yet, at the same time, a person who seeks
conscious understanding may be put off by indirect methods, lose
patience and motivation, and dismiss the experience as useless. Only

experience will teach you to make assessments about which style to use with a particular client.

The second variable to consider in assessing whether to use a direct or indirect style is the degree of responsiveness of the client (or "resistance," traditionally considered a lack of responsiveness). A general guideline that you can use for determining which style to use is this: *The degree of indirection should be directly proportional to the degree of resistance encountered or anticipated* (Zeig, 1980). In other words, the greater the degree of inability or unwillingness to follow the therapist's directions on the part of the client, the more the suggestions should be offered indirectly.

Clinical Demeanor

Before the recent surge of interest in the indirect methods for inducing and utilizing the hypnotic state, the consideration of suggestion style was limited to the demeanor of the clinician while offering direct suggestions. Styles were described on a continuum with "authoritarian" at one extreme and "permissive" at the other. These terms can still be useful in describing the relationship between clinician and client, and so they are included here.

The authoritarian approach is a domineering one in which the clinician literally commands the client to respond in a particular way. Authority and power are the variables the clinician relies on, and the response from the "good" client is compliance.

Authoritarian approaches involve offering suggestions in the form of commands. The following suggestions are structured in an authoritarian mode:

Close your eyes when I count to three.

When I snap my fingers, you will be six years old.

When I touch your shoulder, you will go into a deep state of hypnosis.

You will find it impossible to light a cigarette.

You will not remember anything from this experience.

At the other end of the spectrum is the "permissive" approach, one that is much more respectful of the client's ability to make choices in his or her own behalf about what he or she will and will not respond to. The permissive approach is characterized by its emphasis on allowing the client to become aware of *possibilities* of meaningful responses, rather than making demands for such responses. The following suggestions are structured in a permissive style:

> You may be interested in discovering another way to feel more comfortable.
>
> I wonder whether you have considered the possibility that you might learn these methods more easily than you first thought.
>
> I don't know what the most comfortable position is for you to sit in.
>
> Perhaps you could focus more easily with your eyes closed.
>
> You can choose to listen, if you'd like to, to the things I describe.

The clinician simply offers suggestions of what the client *may* experience *if* he or she chooses to. The responsibility is on the client to a considerable extent to make use in her own way of information that has been provided by the clinician. Therefore, any response is deemed an adequate one by the clinician, respectful of the person's choice. In this way, "resistance" is much less debilitating a factor (Gilligan, 1987; Gordon & Meyers-Anderson, 1981; Grinder & Bandler, 1981; Haley, 1985; Stanton, 1985).

SUGGESTION STRUCTURES

Along with a style for offering suggestions, you must also choose a particular structure of the suggestion. Suggestion structures can take a number of different forms, described below.

Positive suggestions

Positive suggestions are by far the most common, simple, and useful type of suggestion structure. Positive suggestions are supportive and encouraging, and are phrased in such a way as to give the client the idea that he or she can experience or accomplish something desirable. Since words call to mind the experiences that the words (as symbols of experiences) represent, positive suggestions are phrased to create desirable responses. The following suggestions are structured in a positive way (and permissively as well):

> You can feel more comfortable with each breath you inhale.
>
> You can remember a time when you felt very proud of yourself.
>
> You are able to discover inner strengths you didn't realize you had.

You can notice how good it feels to relax.

You may notice a soothing feeling of warmth in your hands.

Negative suggestions

Negative suggestions employ a sort of "reverse psychology" approach when they are used skillfully. Negative suggestions may obtain a response by suggesting the person *not* respond in the desired way.

When used deliberately and in a skilled way, negative suggestions can be most worthwhile. The following are examples of negative suggestions. Notice what your internal experience is as you slowly read each of them.

Do not think of your favorite color.

Do not allow yourself to wonder what time it is.

I would suggest that you not notice that sensation in your leg.

You shouldn't be thinking about your high school sweetheart right now.

Please try not to notice which of your friends is the most materialistic.

All too often, negative suggestions are employed naively and accidentally, generating an undesired response that may leave the practitioner wondering what went wrong. If a clinician says (with great sincerity and with the intention of comforting the client), "Don't worry about it, just put it out of your mind," the client is then most probably going to still worry and think about "it."

Content suggestions

Content suggestions contain very specific details describing feelings, memories, thoughts, or fantasies the client is to experience while in hypnosis. Providing details that describe every dimension of the suggested experience can have the desired effect of assisting the client to have the experience more completely and, therefore, to a greater degree of satisfaction. Examples of content suggestions may include:

Think of a red rose with soft, velvet petals and a gentle, sweet fragrance.

Imagine being at the beach on a bright, clear day, feeling the sun warming your skin, smelling the salt in the ocean breeze, and hearing the pounding of the waves against the shore.

Can you remember how pleasing it is to bite into a juicy orange, how
your mouth waters, and the juice runs all over your fingers, and
how tart it tastes?

Each of the above examples provides specific details about what you
are to experience in thinking of a rose, the beach, or an orange. Perhaps
those details allow you to have the experience more fully, in which case
they are helpful. However, these examples can also illustrate a potential
hazard of using content-filled suggestions, namely that the details I
directed you to notice may not be the ones you would have chosen.

The potential problem with content suggestions is simply this: The
more details you provide, the greater the probability that something you
say will contradict a client's experience (Grinder & Bandler, 1981;
O'Hanlon, 1993).

Process suggestions

In contrast to the detailed content suggestions, process suggestions
are quite sparse on detail, leaving the client free to attend to whatever
details he or she has associated to (i.e., projected into) the suggested
experience.

Process instructions give clients the opportunity to use their own
experience and details in the process, and therefore make what seems at
first glance to be too general to be effective become a highly individualized approach. The following are examples of process instructions:

You can have a particular memory from childhood, one that you
haven't thought about in a long, long time.

You might notice a certain pleasant sensation in your body as you sit
there comfortably.

You may become aware of a specific sound in the room.

Can you remember that special time when you felt so good about
yourself?

None of the above suggestions specifies anything—they do not say
which memory, sensation, sound, or event. The client chooses that
aspect of the experience. Notice, though, that the use of qualifiers such
as "particular," "certain," "specific," and "special" can be employed to
have the client sift all of his or her experience down to one to focus on.
Which one the person chooses is a product of the interaction between
conscious and unconscious choices (Erickson & Rossi, 1979; Zeig, 1980).

Posthypnotic suggestions

Posthypnotic suggestions are those given to the client while he or she is in hypnosis about behaviors and feelings he or she is to have in some future context. Posthypnotic suggestions make it possible for the person to carry over into the desired context the new behaviors or understandings acquired during hypnosis. *Posthypnotic suggestions are a necessary part of the therapeutic process if the client is to carry new possibilities into future experiences.* Without them, the learnings acquired during the hypnosis session will most probably be limited to the hypnotic state itself. The reason for this is that hypnotic responses are state-specific, meaning they are associated to one particular internal state. The posthypnotic suggestion permits the newly acquired learning to cross internal boundaries and become available in other states of consciousness. If the client can have the behavior or feeling only while in hypnosis, he or she is still too restricted.

Posthypnotic suggestions are useful to assure that the desired response will become integrated into the person's everyday life, replacing dysfunctional or absent responses. Furthermore, posthypnotic suggestions can also be used to facilitate future hypnotic work by offering the suggestion that in future sessions the client can go into hypnosis more deeply and rapidly (Erickson & Rossi, 1979, 1981; Lankton & Lankton, 1983).

SPECIALIZED SUGGESTIONS

While the suggestion structure and styles described above represent the core of the hypnotic suggestion, there are numerous other forms of suggestion that may be derived from the core components. Some of these are described in this section.

Accessing questions

Questions that encourage the client to respond at an experiential level rather than only a verbal one are known as accessing questions. More than rhetorical questions, accessing questions focus the client on particular aspects of his or her experiences, which are amplified through the way the questions were asked: For example: "Can you recall, vividly, how very soothing and relaxing it is to lie in the warm sun and feel it warming your skin?" Accessing questions have also been called "conversational postulates" (Bandler & Grinder, 1979; Hammond, 1990).

Ambiguous suggestions

You can deliberately use ambiguity in a suggestion in order to encourage the client's projections (similar to the nonspecific "process" suggestion). The ambiguity may surround the desired action on the part of the client or the meaning of the suggestion. For example, to suggest that, "One can be quite ironwilled and hardheaded in such matters" leaves it open to interpretation as to whether the clinician is praising perseverance or criticizing stubbornness (Grinder & Bandler, 1981; O'Hanlon, 1985).

Apposition of opposites

Offering suggestions that create distinct polarities of experience within the client is making use of the apposition of opposites. For example: "As your left hand becomes pleasantly cold and numb, you'll notice your right hand becoming comfortably warm and responsive" (Erickson & Rossi, 1979; Hammond, 1990).

Bind of comparable alternatives

Providing the client with a bind of comparable alternatives creates a "forced choice" situation for the client in which both choices lead to an equally desirable outcome: "Would you enjoy a deep hypnosis experience sitting in *this* chair or in *that* chair?" As long as the client responds within the parameters of the suggestion, the bind exists (Hammond, 1990).

Confusional suggestions

Suggestions that are deliberately constructed to disorient or confuse the client in order to build responsiveness, overload an overly intellectual demeanor, and facilitate dissociation are known as confusional. For example, you can think you consciously understand the point of such suggestions, but your unconscious likes clarity, too, so if you consciously believe that it will consciously work for you in unconsciously structuring the conscious and unconscious patterns for knowing consciously at an unconscious level that you can overload someone's ability to comprehend, then just make sure you use confusion when it is sensible to do so. Embedded within the confusion are some clear, sensible, and meaningful suggestions that can stand out against the backdrop of confusion. More is said about confusional methods in Chapter 16 (Erickson, 1964; Gilligan, 1987; Otani, 1986).

Covering all possibilities

One way to diffuse resistance and maintain responsiveness in the client is to include all his or her possible responses in your suggestion, thus defining any response as a useful, cooperative one: "You may think of an important memory... perhaps one from early in your life... perhaps one from very recently... or perhaps one from somewhere in-between..." Well, what other possibilities are there? Any memory will be from his or her past, obviously, whether recent, immediate, or distant. Thus, any memory retrieved is in line with the suggestion, assuring a positive response (Grinder & Bandler, 1981; Hammond, 1990).

Implied directives

An indirect way to encourage a response is through the use of implied directives. The first part of the suggestion structure is the indirect suggestion to do something from which the second half of the suggestion then directly suggests a response. For example: "When you experience your hand lifting in just a moment (indirect suggestion), you will notice that it feels very, very light (direct suggestion)" (Bandler & Grinder, 1979; Erickson & Rossi, 1975).

Interspersal of suggestions

The frequent repetition of key words or phrases within an ongoing series of suggestions is making use of an interspersal approach. You can use interspersal to deepen the hypnosis, facilitate the experience of a specific hypnotic phenomenon, "seed" (implant) ideas for future reference, and reiterate an important point. For example: "A *deep* thinker, that is, one who *thinks deeply*, can *evolve a deep understanding* of himself or herself in gaining depth of knowledge about suggestion" (Erickson, 1966; Zeig, 1980).

Metaphors

In the literature of clinical hypnosis, metaphors have come to mean stories. Metaphors are an indirect method to achieve a number of goals. They are considered one of the most powerful and gentle means for communicating relevant information to a client, and so are discussed in detail in several later chapters (Barker, 1985; Gordon, 1978; Wallas, 1985).

Paradoxical suggestions

Paradoxical suggestions contain what seem to be, at first glance, incompatible components contained within the same overall suggestion. For example: "You can take *all the time in the world in the next minute* to complete your inner work of integrating your new learning" (Lange, 1988; Seltzer, 1986).

Presuppositions

A presupposition assumes the response will happen—it's simply a matter of when: "How pleasantly surprised will you be when you discover that you understand presuppositions?" (Gordon, 1985; Haley, 1973).

Puns

The use of humor as a reframing device can be a valuable way of engaging the client in the process while simultaneously establishing a friendly and warm emotional association to the hypnosis. For example: "Some people like to do hypnosis in a very predictable rhyming and rhythmic way, but you know and I know that the rhythm method is not very reliable." (Erickson & Rossi, 1979; Zeig, 1980).

Truisms

A truism is a "common sense" observation that appears to be so self-evident as to be virtually undeniable. Truisms are used to build an acceptance of the suggestion that follows it on the basis of the acceptance of the truism: "Every person is unique, we all know that *(truism)*, which is why you can experience deep hypnosis in your own unique way" (Erickson & Rossi, 1979; Hammond, 1990).

CONCLUSION

Words are stimuli, and they come to evoke the same or similar responses as the objects or concepts they represent. Therefore, words have to be chosen carefully, as does the manner in which the words are spoken.

REFERENCES

Alman, B. & Carney, R. (1980). Consequences of direct and indirect suggestions on success of posthypnotic behavior. *American Journal of Clinical Hypnosis, 23,*

112–118.

Bandler, R. & Grinder, J. (1979). *Frogs into princes.* Moab, UT: Real People Press.

Barker, P. (1985). *Using metaphors in psychotherapy.* New York: Brunner/Mazel.

Brown, P. (1991). *The hypnotic brain.* New Haven, CT: Yale University Press.

Crasilneck, H. & Hall, J. (1985) *Clinical hypnosis: Principles and applications.* Orlando: Grune & Stratton.

Erickson, M. (1964). The confusion technique in hypnosis. *American Journal of Clinical Hypnosis, 6,* 183–207.

Erickson, M. (1966). The interspersal hypnotic technique for symptom correction and pain control. *American Journal of Clinical Hypnosis, 8,* 198–209.

Erickson, M. & Rossi, E. (1975). Varieties of double bind. *American Journal of Clinical Hypnosis, 17,* 143–157.

Erickson, M. & Rossi, E. (1979). *Hypnotherapy: An exploratory casebook.* New York: Irvington.

Erickson, M. & Rossi, E. (1981). *Experiencing hypnosis: Therapeutic approaches to altered states.* New York: Irvington.

Gilligan, S. (1987). *Therapeutic trances: The cooperation principle in Ericksonian hypnotherapy.* New York: Brunner/Mazel.

Gordon, D. (1978). *Therapeutic metaphors.* Cupertino, CA: Meta Publications.

Gordon, D. (1985). The role of presuppositions in Ericksonian psychotherapy. In. J. Zeig (Ed.), *Ericksonian psychotherapy: Vol. 1, Structures* (pp. 62–76). New York: Brunner/Mazel.

Gordon, D. & Meyers-Anderson, M. (1981). *Phoenix: Therapeutic patterns of Milton H. Erickson, M.D.* Cupertino, CA: Meta Publications.

Grinder, J. & Bandler, R. (1981). *Trance-formations: Neuro-Linguistic Programming and the structure of hypnosis.* Moab, UT: Real People Press.

Haley, J. (1973). *Uncommon therapy.* New York: Norton.

Haley, J. (Ed.) (1985). *Conversations with Milton H. Erickson, M.D.* (Vol. 1). New York: Triangle Press.

Hammond, D. (Ed.) (1990). *Handbook of hypnotic suggestions and metaphors.* New York: Norton.

Kroger, W. (1977). *Clinical and experimental hypnosis* (2nd ed.). Philadelphia: Lippincott.

Lange, A. (1988). A new way of motivating clients to carry out paradoxical assignments: The combination of the paradoxical and the congruent. In J. Zeig & S. Lankton (Eds.), *Developing Ericksonian therapy: State of the art* (pp. 280–301). New York: Brunner/Mazel.

Lankton, S. & Lankton, C. (1983). *The answer within: A clinical framework of Ericksonian hypnotherapy.* New York: Brunner/Mazel.

Lehrer, M. (1986). How much complexity and indirection are necessary? In B. Zilbergeld, M. Edelstein & D. Araoz (Eds.), *Hypnosis: Questions and answers* (pp. 244–247). New York: Norton.

O'Hanlon, W. (1985). A study guide of frameworks of Milton H. Erickson's hypnosis and therapy. In J. Zeig (Ed.), *Ericksonian psychotherapy: Vol. 1, Structures* (pp. 33-51). New York: Brunner/Mazel.

O'Hanlon, W. & Martin, M. (1993). *Solution-oriented hypnosis.* New York: Norton.

Otani, A. (1989). The confusion technique untangled: Its theoretical rationale and preliminary classification. *American Journal of Clinical Hypnosis, 31*(3), 164–172.

Seltzer, L. (1986). *Paradoxical strategies in psychotherapy.* New York: John Wiley & Sons.

Spiegel, H. & Spiegel, D. (1987). *Trance and treatment: Clinical uses of hypnosis.* Washington, DC: American Psychiatric Press.

Stanton, H. (1985). Permissive vs. authoritarian approaches in clinical and experimental settings. In J. Zeig (Ed.), *Ericksonian psychotherapy: Vol. 1, Structures* (pp. 293–304). New York: Brunner/Mazel.

Wallas, L. (1985). *Stories for the third ear: Using hypnotic fables in psychotherapy.* New York: Norton.

Weitzenhoffer, A. (1989). *The practice of hypnotism* (Vols. 1&2). New York: John Wiley & Sons.

Yapko, M. (1983). A comparative analysis of direct and indirect hypnotic communication styles. *American Journal of Clinical Hypnosis, 25,* 270–276.

Zeig, J. (Ed.) (1980). *A teaching seminar with Milton H. Erickson, M.D.* New York: Brunner/Mazel.

Zeig, J. & Rennick, P. (1991). Ericksonian hypnotherapy: A communications approach to hypnosis. In S. Lynn & J. Rhue (Eds.), *Theories of hypnosis: Current models and perspectives* (pp. 275–300). New York: Guilford.

13

PATTERNS OF HYPNOTIC COMMUNICATION

In this chapter, general guidelines for choosing the particular words and phrases you intend to use in your hypnosis session will be provided. These guidelines are intended to assist you in formulating suggestions that are more likely to be accepted by the individual you are working with.

KEEP THE SUGGESTIONS SIMPLE AND EASY TO FOLLOW

Generally, the more complicated a set of instructions for someone to follow, the more the person must rely on the conscious mind to help sort things out. The more the person must rely on the conscious mind, the less the unconscious mind is accessible, essentially defeating the purpose of doing hypnosis. Keeping suggestions relatively simple allows your client to flow with the process without having to critically, and, therefore, consciously, analyze, interpret, and judge the offered suggestions.

USE YOUR CLIENT'S LANGUAGE

I have described how words represent experiences, and even though we use a common language, our internal experiences are necessarily different. Taking the client's words, then attaching *your* meaning to them, then translating them into the language *you* use, and communicating from your linguistic style are all steps that are arbitrary on your part, and are more likely to lead to miscommunication.

In using the language of the client, you do not assume even for a moment that you mean the same thing as he or she does in using it. You can use the same language as your client because it is his or her world you are dealing with—not yours (O'Hanlon, 1987; Sherman, 1988).

HAVE THE CLIENT DEFINE EVERYTHING IN EXPERIENTIAL TERMS

Since words are symbols of experience, using the same words does not mean you are describing the same experience. Therefore, it is important to have the client explain the experience as best as possible, rather than just using a word or two to represent the experience. Any words used will never completely give you an idea of what the person is subjectively experiencing, but the more definition and description of his or her experience you have, the more opportunity you have for meaningful intervention (Bandler & Grinder, 1979; Zeig, 1980).

USE THE PRESENT TENSE AND A POSITIVE STRUCTURE

Generally, suggestions should be phrased in the present tense and in term of what the person is experiencing. Of course, most therapeutic suggestions are intended to include future behavior in some way, but the hypnotic session is the bridge between what is now and what will be then. The basic structure of hypnotic suggestions is linking ("chaining") what is occurring now with what is desired: "As you experience this, you can start to experience that." Continuous feedback about the person's present state is necessary to make the bridge effective.

In general, suggestions should be phrased in positive ways about what the person *can* do instead of what he or she *can't* do (Grinder & Bandler, 1981; Hammond, 1990).

ENCOURAGE AND REINFORCE THE CLIENT

In my view, the process of encouraging clients is often one of guiding them into a position where they can acknowledge personal strengths and resources previously overlooked in themselves (Erickson & Rossi, 1979; Hammond, 1990).

DETERMINE OWNERSHIP OF THE PROBLEM

Different therapeutic approaches have different terminology to express this concept, each one addressing the need to guide the client into accepting a measure of responsibility for what he or she is experiencing. Helping people discover that they have power, at most, to control the events in their lives, or at least, their reactions to the events in their lives is a necessary component of therapeutic work (Ellis, 1987; Walter & Peller, 1992).

DETERMINE THE BEST MODALITY FOR THE HYPNOTIC EXPERIENCE

One of the most useful concepts originating from Richard Bandler and John Grinder's Neuro-Linguistic Programming (NLP) model concerns people's preferred style for gathering information, storing it, retrieving it, and communicating about it.

It is important to realize that each person processes experience in all of the (intact) senses all of the time. The issue of concern here is which modality is dominant in a given context. If a clinician can identify a person's favored system of sensory experiences, he or she can adapt communications to that favored system and increase the likelihood of meaningful influence through the attainment of greater rapport.

The language a person uses, particularly the predicates (including verbs, adverbs, and adjectives), reflects a person's favored information-processing modality, and hypnotic processes can be worded accordingly (Yapko, 1981).

The sensory language used in your hypnotic process will orient your client to one or more of their senses. The primary modalities of hypnotic processes are visual, auditory, and kinesthetic. Olfactory and gustatory experiences can be integrated into the kinesthetic category.

If, for example, you wanted to orient someone to the visual portion of an experience, you would intersperse visually based terminology, as in the following:

> *Picture* yourself at the beach...get a clear *image* of the shore-line...*looking* out over the ocean to the horizon...*seeing* the silhouettes of sailboats in the distance...enjoying the relaxing *images* of the sun sparkling on the water's surface...

To orient your client to the auditory component of experience, you would intersperse auditory based terminology, as in the following:

> Now, I don't know what you *tell* yourself...when you're *saying* things to yourself through your thoughts...but that internal *dialogue* plays a large role in the overall quality of your experience...and it would be nice to *hear you tell yourself* some positive things...complimentary things...

The kinesthetic portion of experiences encompasses feelings as well as tactile experiences. Thus, to absorb a client in kinesthetic experiences means using the language of feelings, as in the following:

> When you recalled that *happy* memory a moment ago...your whole demeanor changed...it was obviously a *wonderful* feeling...to *feel* loved...to *sense* the deep appreciation for you...so *strong* and so obvious almost as if you could *touch* it...and that is a powerful *emotional* experience...that you can *hold onto* for the rest of your life...

As a general principle, the more you focus your clients on aspects of experience they don't normally notice, the more valuable they will find the process. Therapy often involves developing underdeveloped parts of oneself and "tuning in" to things previously "tuned out."

KEEP THE CLIENT ONLY AS INFORMED AS IS NECESSARY TO SUCCEED

While I have made it a high priority to provide relevant information to clients, it is also necessary not to provide too much information about your interventions. Giving the client the opportunity to develop defenses by analyzing and criticizing what the clinician is doing can be counterproductive to the aims of therapy.

The idea of presenting and withholding information selectively can be an ethical dilemma. How can a client provide informed consent if he or she doesn't know what the clinician is doing? Yet, if he or she knows exactly what the clinician is doing, how can some interventions, especially strategic ones, succeed? This is a matter that must be handled delicately on a case-by-case basis (Booth, 1988; Frauman, Lynn & Brentar, 1993).

GIVE YOUR CLIENTS THE TIME THEY NEED TO RESPOND

We all do things according to our own internal time clock, our own pace. In hypnosis, this tendency is amplified to the point of being a critical component of the interaction. To pressure someone to respond to *your* pace of doing things just won't work in doing hypnosis. Instead, allow the client to form the desired response at a rate he or she chooses (Erickson & Rossi, 1979).

GET PERMISSION BEFORE TOUCHING YOUR CLIENTS

I have seen many sessions that were going well ruined in an instant because the clinician assumed enough rapport was present (if he or she even thought about it, which a lot of "touchey-feeley" clinicians never do) to touch the person. It is very important to get permission to touch the client before doing so for a number of reasons.

First of all, touch is something related to intimacy—a cross into personal space. Some welcome it, while others hate to be touched by strangers and experience it as a violation of personal territory. With such persons, touching can hinder rapport, not help.

Second, in the hypnotic state the person is typically focused inwardly on some internal experience. To respond to a clinician's touch means reorienting your focus to the external world, which is generally counterproductive to the development and maintenance of a deep hypnotic state. If you use touch indiscriminately, you can unintentionally work against yourself.

Whether you ask before you begin hypnosis or at some time during the session is a matter of personal preference (I prefer to do both). By securing permission before touching your client, you will demonstrate your respect for his or her integrity.

ESTABLISH ANTICIPATION SIGNALS

Anticipation signals are statements of your intentions, effectively letting your clients know what action you are going to take so as to not startle them. They also serve the function of keeping clients comfortable enough to not feel like they have to pay conscious attention to everything you say and do. Such conscious analysis is counterproductive.

Anticipation signals take the form of simple statements about what is coming next. When you state, "In just a moment I'm going to..." and then follow through in a way that is consistent with what you stated your actions would be, a new level of trust can be reached, aiding in future work. From the client's perspective, it is very difficult to be relaxed and on guard simultaneously. Anticipation signals are a quick, simple way to foster trust in the hypnotic relationship.

USE A VOICE AND DEMEANOR CONSISTENT WITH YOUR INTENT

It helps immeasurably to have control of your voice and body in communicating, using yourself as the mechanism to drive a suggestion home. To have tension in your voice when you suggest to your client that he or she relax is an avoidable incongruity. To use a normal conversational tone of voice with someone you are wanting to guide into a different state of experience is another avoidable incongruity. Using a soothing, comforting voice also serves the purpose of discouraging conscious analysis (Bandler & Grinder, 1979; Gilligan, 1987).

CHAIN SUGGESTIONS STRUCTURALLY

In using the phrase "chaining suggestions," I am referring to the chaining of the desired response to the client's present experience. Bandler and Grinder's "pacing and leading" (1979) and Erickson & Rossi's "accepting and utilizing" (1979) principles are synonymous with "chaining." The idea is to build a link (hence "chain") between what the client is currently doing and what you would like him or her to do. The implicit message is, "As you experience (this), you can start to experience (that)." For example, sitting there and reading these words will allow you to think of your left foot.

These links are the basis for the hypnotic process being a flowing one rather than a choppy, disconnected one. Hypnotic phrasing is a strict grammarian's nightmare, but to the person in hypnosis the clinician is smooth and easy to listen to (Hammond, 1990; O'Hanlon, 1985).

BE GENERAL SPECIFICALLY

If you refer back to the section on process suggestion structures, you can review the general idea that the more details you provide for someone's hypnotic experience, the more opportunities there are for contradicting it. For example, "Let your right hand feel warmer" as a suggestion for the specific response of hand warmth is easier to resist than is a more general process suggestion: "Let yourself notice the particular change of temperature in one of your hands." In the latter suggestion, which hand was to change was not specified, nor was it specific whether the hand was to grow warmer or cooler. Whatever response the person has can now be defined as a cooperative one, and is recognized as a projection of the person's unconscious associations (Grinder & Bandler, 1981; Watzlawick, 1978).

CONCLUSION

While this chapter covered some of the basic components of hypnotic communication, it obviously could not cover all the subtleties inherent in such patterns. You may be reminded that for each general principle discussed, there are exceptions.

REFERENCES

Bandler, R. & Grinder, J. (1979). *Frogs into princes.* Moab, UT: Real People Press.

Booth, P. (1988). Strategic therapy revisited. In J. Zeig & S. Lankton (Eds.), *Developing Ericksonian therapy: State of the art* (pp. 39–58). New York: Brunner/Mazel.

Ellis, A. (1987). The evolution of Rational-Emotive Therapy (RET) and Cognitive-Behavioral Therapy (CBT). In *The evolution of psychotherapy* (pp. 107–125). New York: Brunner/Mazel.

Erickson, M. & Rossi, E. (1979). *Hypnotherapy: An exploratory casebook.* New York: Irvington.

Frauman, D., Lynn, S. & Brentar, J. (1993). Prevention and therapeutic management of "negative effects" in hypnotherapy. In J. Rhue, S. Lynn & I. Kirsch (Eds.), *Handbook of clinical hypnosis* (pp. 95–120). Washington, DC: American Psychological Association.

Gilligan, S. (1987). *Therapeutic trances: The cooperation principle in Ericksonian hypnotherapy.* New York: Brunner/Mazel.

Grinder, J. & Bandler, R. (1981). *Trance-formations: Neuro-Linguistic Programming and the structure of hypnosis.* Moab, UT: Real People Press.

Hammond, D. (Ed.) (1990). *Handbook of hypnotic suggestions and metaphors.* New York: Norton.

O'Hanlon, W. (1985). A study guide for frameworks of Milton H. Erickson's hypnosis and therapy. In J. Zeig (Ed.), *Ericksonian psychotherapy: Vol. 1, Structures* (pp. 33–51). New York: Brunner/Mazel.

O'Hanlon, W. (1987). *Taproots: Underlying principles of Milton Erickson's therapy and hypnosis.* New York: Norton.

Seligman, M. (1975). *Helplessness: On depression, development and health.* San Francisco: W. H. Freeman.

Sherman, S. (1988). Ericksonian psychotherapy and social psychology. In J. Zeig & S. Lankton (Eds.), *Developing Ericksonian therapy: State of the art* (pp. 59–90). New York: Brunner/Mazel.

Walter, J. & Peller, J. (1992). *Becoming solution-focused in brief therapy.* New York: Brunner/Mazel.

Watzlawick, P. (1978). *The language of change.* New York: Basic Books.

Yapko, M. (1981). The effect of matching primary representational system predicates on hypnotic relaxation. *American Journal of Clinical Hypnosis, 23,* 169–175.

Zeig, J. (Ed.) (1980). *A teaching seminar with Milton H. Erickson, M.D.* New York: Brunner/Mazel.

14

SUGGESTIBILITY TESTS

For more traditionally oriented clinicians, the use of hypnosis is often predicated on the ideas that only some people are hypnotizable and that people are hypnotizable to varying degrees. From their perspective, tests are viewed as a desirable way to assess *whether* someone is hypnotizable, and, if so, to what degree. I do not use formal suggestibility tests in my practice; instead, I assume the inevitable presence of suggestibility on the part of my client. For the hypnotist who does not share this perspective, or for the hypnotist who does not yet feel experienced enough to assess a client's spontaneous communications for suggestibility dynamics, suggestibility tests may be a useful tool.

Suggestibility tests in clinical practice generally take the form of mini-hypnotic encounters in which a brief, ritualized set of suggestions for relaxation are offered to the client, followed by a suggestion for a specific response. If the client responds in the manner suggested, he or she has "passed" the test. More tests may follow, each one (according to traditional thought) requiring a greater degree of hypnotic depth in order to provide the suggested response. If the client does not respond in the manner suggested, then he or she has "failed" the test. The quality of the client's response (i.e., opposite, minimal) should be noted for informational purposes about this person's response style; thus, potentially useful information can be obtained even from a poor suggestibility test performance (Weitzenhoffer, 1989).

FUNCTIONS OF SUGGESTIBILITY TESTS

The chief purpose of suggestibility tests is to determine the client's degree, if any, of hypnotizability. However, suggestibility tests can also serve a number of other purposes. First, by using suggestibility tests to measure hypnotic responsiveness, valuable information can be obtained regarding which approach may be best for a particular client.

Specifically, should the approach be a direct or indirect one? Should suggestions be in a positive or negative form? Should the hypnotist's demeanor be a commanding, authoritarian one, or an easygoing, permissive one? Much emphasis has been placed on the relationship dynamics between the clinician and client, and suggestibility tests may be a useful tool to help you assess the style you will use to approach a particular client.

A second purpose of the suggestibility test is to serve as a conditioning experience for entering hypnosis. Future hypnotic experiences will involve many of the same dynamics to a greater degree, and so the suggestibility test may be a useful "rehearsal" for the client (Spiegel & Spiegel, 1987).

A third purpose of the suggestibility test can be its ability to accomplish what I call "pre-work work." If the suggestibility test is introduced as preliminary to the "real" therapeutic work to be done, it can be an opportunity to catch the client off guard and offer some therapeutic suggestions that may be less subject to critical analysis by the client (Bates, 1993).

PERFORMING SUGGESTIBILITY TESTS

Introducing and performing the suggestibility test require as much skill in communication as any other dimension of working with hypnosis. There are the matters of timing (i.e., when in the relationship it is introduced), the explanation of its role, the style in which it is offered, the clinician's response to the client's response, and the closure and transition to the next phase of interaction.

Here are some of the more commonly used suggestibility tests:

Chevreul's Pendulum

A pendulum is given to the subject with the instruction to hold the chain between thumb and forefinger. You now begin to use suggestions to suggest and amplify nonvolitional movement of the pendulum. The greater the degree of the pendulum's swing, the greater the degree of suggestibility.

Arm Levitation

The arm levitation and catalepsy technique involves offering the client suggestions that his or her arm begins to feel so light, so weightless, that it begins to lift off his or her lap effortlessly (Kirsch, Lynn & Rhue, 1993).

The Coue Hand Clasp

The subject is requested to sit comfortably, hands together and fingers interlaced. Some suggestions are offered about his or her hands being stuck (tied, glued...) together. It is further suggested that the harder he or she tries to pull them apart the more tightly stuck together they become. The client is then challenged to pull his or her hands apart. Failure to do so indicates suggestibility (Cohen, 1984).

Eye Closure and Catalepsy

In this technique, the "try vs. do" formula ("The harder you try, the more difficult it will be... Now try... Now you can... Go ahead and do...") is applied to eye closure. Suggestions are given that the person's eyes are so heavy they will close, and that the muscles of the eyes are so relaxed and limp that he or she cannot open them. The harder he or she tries to open them, the more tightly closed they become (Weitzenhoffer, 1989).

The Hot Object Technique

In this technique, the subject is given an object to hold in her hand which she is told is going to begin to heat up. The length of time it takes to "heat up" and the degree of hot sensation associated with it are the measures of suggestibility in this test (Hilgard, 1965).

Embedded Commands

Embedded commands are suggestions for specific responses that are embedded in the context of a larger communication, and therefore can escape conscious detection. For example, if I use my voice to accent slightly (e.g., through a change of voice or volume) the italicized words in the following question, I am embedding a suggestion for a specific response.

"Isn't it nice to... *close your eyes* ... at the end of the day?" I may get the eye closure response, an obvious indicator of suggestibility.

More spontaneous, less imposing and arbitrary, embedded commands can be a more useful indicator of suggestibility because of their subtlety (Grinder & Bandler, 1981; Hammond, 1990).

Nonverbal Shifts

Part of attaining rapport is the "pacing" or "mirroring" of client behaviors outside of their consciousness. By matching clients' breathing pattern, for example, you will have mirrored a part of them that is not in their awareness. If you then shift your breathing and theirs follows, they are responding to you unconsciously — an indicator of rapport and suggestibility (Zeig, 1985).

REFERENCES

Bates, B. (1993). Individual differences in response to hypnosis. In J. Rhue, S. Lynn & I. Kirsch (Eds.), *Handbook of clinical hypnosis* (pp. 23–54). Washington, DC: American Psychological Association.

Coe, W. (1993). Expectations and hypnotherapy. In J. Rhue, S. Lynn & I. Kirsch (Eds.), *Handbook of clinical hypnosis* (pp. 73–93). Washington, DC: American Psychological Association.

Cohen, S. (1984). Tests of susceptibility/hypnotizability. In W. Wester & A. Smith (Eds.) *Clinical hypnosis: A multidisciplinary approach* (pp. 73–81). Philadelphia: Lippincott.

Grinder, J. & Bandler, R. (1981). *Trance-formations: Neuro-Linguistic Programming and the structure of hypnosis.* Moab, UT: Real People Press.

Hammond, D. (Ed.) (1990). *Handbook of hypnotic suggestions and metaphors.* New York: Norton.

Hilgard, E. (1965). *The experience of hypnosis.* New York: Harcourt, Brace & World.

Kirsch, I., Lynn, S. & Rhue, J. (1993). Introduction to clinical hypnosis. In J. Rhue, S. Lynn & I. Kirsch (Eds.), *Handbook of clinical hypnosis* (pp. 3–22). Washington, DC: American Psychological Association.

Spiegel, H. & Spiegel, D. (1987). *Trance and treatment: Clinical uses of hypnosis.* Washington, DC: American Psychiatric Press.

Weitzenhoffer, A. (1989). *The practice of hypnotism* (Vol. 1). New York: John Wiley & Sons.

Zeig, J. (1985). Therapeutic patterns of Ericksonian influence communication. In J. Zeig (Ed.), *The evolution of psychotherapy* (pp. 392–406). New York: Brunner/Mazel.

15

INDUCING THE FORMAL HYPNOTIC STATE

This chapter considers the second phase of the hypnotic interaction, the hypnotic induction and the intensifying ("deepening") of the hypnotic state. The induction serves several purposes:

1. It provides a concrete stimulus for the client to focus his or her attention on, serving as a bridge between the "normal waking state" and the hypnotic state (Spiegel & Spiegel, 1987).
2. It occupies the conscious mind, and in so doing dissociates it while amplifying the unconscious mind's associational abilities. This is the chief function of an induction—facilitating the dissociation of conscious and unconscious. The degree of dissociation obtained is the general measure of the depth of the experience (Watzlawick, 1978; Zeig, 1980).
3. It allows for the building of a "response set," a characteristic pattern for responding to the guidance of the clinician (Erickson & Rossi, 1979; Hammond, 1990).

The hypnotic induction as the stimulus of the hypnotic experience obviously plays a pivotal role in the overall quality of the interaction. There are as many inductions as there are practitioners of hypnosis, and since it is neither practical nor desirable to list them all I have included only several of the more useful and common ones. I have divided the inductions into two general categories: traditional inductions and the utilization approach to induction. This chapter will present some of the traditional inductions; the utilization approaches are discussed in the next chapter.

TRADITIONAL HYPNOTIC INDUCTIONS

In using the term "traditional" to describe the inductions presented in this chapter, I have two meanings. The first application is for the literal translation of the word "traditional." These techniques have been used effectively for a very long time, handed down from generation to generation of hypnotists. The second is for the association of the traditional model of hypnosis described earlier in which the process of induction is a highly directive and ritualistic one. The traditional model presupposes the necessity of a formal ritual in order for hypnosis to occur, which is an unnecessarily limiting perspective.

Each of these traditional inductions has key phrases and key concepts that are integral to the technique and these must necessarily be present in order for the technique to be employed. These techniques are invaluable in the practice of clinical hypnosis, and should be mastered as basic skills in hypnosis. In presenting these techniques at this point, the assumption is that there has been ample opportunity to have developed enough sensitivity to communication variables to appreciate that, as structured as these techniques are, they will need to be varied from client to client (Weitzenhoffer, 1989).

Beginning the Induction of Hypnosis

In beginning the induction, generally there are certain minimal responses you will want from your client. Suggesting, directly or indirectly, that the client assume a comfortable physical position is a good starting point. The general immobility (catalepsy) and the extra effort it takes to readjust one's position while in hypnosis make it worthwhile to be sure the client is in a position he or she can stay in effortlessly over time. A second consideration may be to suggest a comfortable rate of breathing; you may notice with experience that anticipation and fascination often lead the client to breathe irregularly and even hold breaths unconsciously. A third consideration is suggesting the client close his or her eyes at the start in order to begin to build an internal focus (Coe, 1993).

With the client comfortable and growing increasingly responsive to the clinician, the induction is under way. Here, then, are specific techniques for facilitating hypnosis.

Progressive Muscle Relaxation Techniques

The progressive muscle relaxation technique involves offering suggestions of relaxation of the various muscle groups of the body sequentially. The body is divided into as few or as many specific muscle groups as you wish depending on how long or short you think the process need be (Kirsch, Lynn & Rhue, 1993).

Over time, the association of relaxation is formed to your mere mention of bodily relaxation; thus, after a short while of the client practicing this technique, the relaxation response can come quite quickly.

A second variation on the progressive muscle relaxation technique involves the same principle. By using a countdown (associating a number to each muscle group, e.g., "10...relax your feet...9...relax your calves and shins...") as part of the process, you can in later sessions simply count downward in the conditioned sequence and each number will trigger the associated relaxation response for that particular muscle group.

A third variation of this technique is called the "Deep Muscle Relaxation" technique. In this technique, the progression through the body is the same, but the client is instructed to deliberately tense the muscles of the specific group under consideration. Have the client hold the tension in the muscles for 10 seconds or so, and then release it. The relaxation of the muscles is both immediate and substantial.

Relaxed Scene Experience

This technique involves offering suggestions to clients of experiencing themselves in some special place where they can feel very relaxed, secure, and happy. As details of the place are described, clients can experience more and more of themselves there.

Anywhere clients can feel comfortable is sufficient in order for this technique to be effective. In the event that clients do not have a place in their experience where they felt good to go to, they can then *imagine* such a place; almost all people have some fantasy place they would like to travel to (Smith & Wester, 1984).

Eye Fixation

If not the oldest, certainly one of the oldest, techniques for inducing hypnosis is the classic "eye fixation" method. This technique involves having the client fixate his or her gaze on some specific stimulus. The stimulus can be virtually anything: a spot on the ceiling or wall, the clinician's thumb, a dangling watch or crystal ball, a fireplace, a candle, a fishtank, an hourglass, whatever. *Anything* that holds the client's attention long enough for him or her to respond to the simultaneous suggestions for relaxation will suffice in this technique.

As the client stares at the stimulus, suggestions are offered to notice every observable detail and, while fixing his or her gaze, to experience growing more relaxed.

Commenting on the client's blinking, pacing your words to the eye blinks, and even modeling eye closure can further suggest desired responses (Coe, 1993).

Counting Methods

Counting methods of induction generally involve counting downward (implying "going down" deeper into hypnosis) while offering suggestions of relaxation and comfort between numbers (Miller, 1979).

The "As If" Method

Generally a good method for more "difficult" clients, this pattern involves no direct suggestion to the client to respond in a particular way, but rather a suggestion to act "as if" he or she were responding in the way suggested. In terms of the outcome, where the act ends and the reality begins is ambiguous since the responses are identical.

Suggesting that a client act "as if" he or she is comfortable, relaxed, thinking about a happy moment, or whatever paves the way for the client to really experience those suggestions without any actual personal demands being made (Grinder & and Bandler, 1981).

INTENSIFYING (DEEPENING) TECHNIQUES

The deepening techniques presented in this section are techniques that have been traditionally used in order to intensify the client's hypnotic state after the formal induction has been administered.

The Stairs (Or Elevator) Going Down

In this deepening technique, the client is told to imagine (i.e., see, hear, feel) himself or herself at the top of a flight of "special stairs" or on a "special elevator." As he or she experiences herself going *down* the stairs one relaxing step at a time, he or she can go down deeper into hypnosis. Or, as each floor is passed in the descending elevator, he or she can experience himself or herself going deeper into hypnosis (Smith & Wester, 1984).

Compounding

In the chapter on basic communication patterns of hypnosis, I discussed "chaining," also called "verbal compounding," which is the tying of one suggestion to another according to the formula "As you X, you can Y" (e.g., "As you read this, you can begin to understand compounding").Verbal compounding serves as a deepener by continually building new responses on the framework of past responses, thus intensifying the hypnotic experience.

"Manual Compounding" is the tying of verbal suggestions to physical experience. As a deepener, it can take the form of offering suggestions of going deeper into hypnosis while experiencing physical sensations that reinforce the suggestions (e.g., "As your arm drops slowly to your side, you drop more deeply into hypnosis").

The Mind's Eye Closure

This technique involves offering suggestions about the presence of the "mind's eye" as that part of the mind that remains active in thinking and imaging as the induction progresses. With suggestions for the "mind's eyelid," similar to the "Eye Fixation" suggestions of the "eyelids getting heavy," the client can slowly close out stray thoughts and images and experience a deeper state of hypnosis.

This technique can be an effective way of "turning off" much of the internal dialogue that goes on continuously in each of us, making hypnosis easier to experience.

Silence

Silence can be a useful deepening technique if used skillfully. Following an induction, suggestions can be offered to the effect that the client can now "have some silent time to enjoy the relaxation of hypnosis while deepening the experience."

Posthypnotic Suggestion and Re-Induction

This deepening technique, also called "Refractionation," involves giving the client already in hypnosis a posthypnotic suggestion that the next time hypnosis is reinduced, he or she can go into hypnosis both more deeply and more quickly. The clinician then guides the person in and out of hypnosis several times within the same session (Gilligan, 1987; Werner, 1984). This is an excellent technique for those with a short attention span for whatever reason (i.e., attention deficit disorder, physical pain, depression, or whatever else might impair one's ability to focus).

SUMMARY

Presented in this chapter were some of the most common and useful methods for inducing and deepening the hypnotic state according to traditional, structured approaches. *Anything* that focuses the person's attention and facilitates feelings of comfort and well-being can be used as an induction. Those presented here are intended to provide a basic foundation on which to build.

REFERENCES

Coe, W. (1993). Expectations and hypnotherapy. In J. Rhue, S. Lynn & I. Kirsch (Eds.), *Handbook of clinical hypnosis* (pp. 73–94). Washington, DC: American Psychological Association.

Erickson, M. & Rossi, E. (1979). *Hypnotherapy: An exploratory casebook.* New York: Irvington.

Gilligan, S. (1987). *Therapeutic trances: The cooperation principle in Ericksonian hypnotherapy.* New York: Brunner/Mazel.

Grinder, J. & Bandler, R. (1981). *Trance-formations: Neuro-Linguistic Programming and the structure of hypnosis.* Moab, UT: Real People Press.

Hammond, D. (Ed.) (1990). *Handbook of hypnotic suggestions and metaphors.* New York: Norton.

Kirsch, I., Lynn, S. & Rhue, J. (1993). Introduction to clinical hypnosis. In J. Rhue, S. Lynn & I. Kirsch (Eds.), *Handbook of clinical hypnosis* (pp. 3–22). Washington, DC: American Psychological Association.

Miller, M. (1979). *Therapeutic hypnosis.* New York: Human Sciences Press.

Smith, A. & Wester, W. (1984). Techniques of induction and deepening. In W. Wester & A. Smith (Eds.), *Clinical hypnosis: A multidisciplinary approach* (pp. 42–72). Philadelphia: Lippincott.

Spiegel, H. & Spiegel, D. (1987). *Trance and treatment: Clinical uses of hypnosis.* Washington, DC: American Psychiatric Press.

Watzlawick, P. (1978). *The language of change.* New York: Basic Books.

Weitzenhoffer, A. (1989). *The practice of hypnotism* (Vol. 1). New York: John Wiley & Sons.

Werner, T. (1984). Hypnosis in psychiatry. In W. Wester & A. Smith (Eds.), *Clinical hypnosis: A multidisciplinary approach* (pp. 353–367). Philadelphia: Lippincott.

Zeig, J. (Ed.) (1980). *A teaching seminar with Milton H. Erickson, M.D.* New York: Brunner/Mazel.

16

NATURALISTIC HYPNOTIC INDUCTIONS

The structured hypnotic inductions presented in the previous chapter are based on the general assumption that hypnosis is a special, if not artificial, state.

In the utilization approach, hypnosis is not considered either an extraordinary or artificially created phenomenon. Rather, hypnosis is viewed as natural experience occurring routinely in almost all people. In adopting this perspective, the skilled clinician must recognize hypnotic responses as they naturally occur in the course of clinical interaction and then build on them meaningfully. In other words, the skilled clinician can create hypnotic responses from hypnotic patterns of communication that capture the client's attention and focus him or her on experiences that will be therapeutically significant. The instructions to the client in this approach are typically more process-oriented than content-filled. There is often not as clear a beginning, middle, or end to the induction relative to the clearer transitions of the more structured, content-oriented approaches of the previous chapter (Erickson, 1958; Haley, 1973).

Securing and maintaining the attention of the client is a beginning point for the hypnotic interaction. Talking meaningfully about the issues that brought the person into treatment, telling absorbing stories that parallel the client's experience, and behaving in unexpected ways are three common techniques for securing attention. As the client's attention is drawn to the clinician, building on the client's responses by acknowledging them and then suggesting (directly or indirectly) that he or she can expand himself or herself further makes use of the client's attentiveness. When the clinician notices hypnotic responses building (absorption, changes in breathing, a fixed posture, muscular tension dissipating, etc.), he or she can begin to engage the person in the process of hypnotic induction and deepening through the naturalistic techniques described in this chapter (Lynn, Neufeld & Matyi, 1987; O'Hanlon, 1987; Otani, 1989a; Zeig & Rennick, 1991).

NATURALISTIC INDUCTIONS

Using Past Hypnotic Experiences

The induction technique of "Using Past Hypnotic Experiences" involves the following two general categories of previous experiences on which to build: 1) informal experiences with hypnosis that people may have during the normal course of daily living without realizing they are hypnotic; and, 2) formal experiences with hypnosis, specifically the previous time(s) the client experienced hypnosis successfully. Either approach may be offered in a process-oriented or content-filled structure, described later in this section.

In the approach building on informal experience with hypnosis, the phase of attentional absorption typically involves some preinduction discussion about the nature of hypnosis while exploring the client's association to hypnosis. At some point, the clinician can begin to model attentiveness, immobility, and slowed breathing, and can begin to hypnotically describe one or more natural situations in which hypnosis occurs. Such situations might include long drives, absorption in a good book or movie, having a massage or jacuzzi, daydreaming, praying, and any other situation where the person has had the experience of being absorbed or focused intently. The nonverbal shift from a routine conversational tone of voice and pace to one that is slower, quieter, and more meaningfully articulated is fundamental to guiding the person into the suggested memory of that natural hypnotic state he or she has previously experienced. Through the absorption in that memory, hypnotic responses (i.e., the ideodynamics) begin to arise in the here-and-now, which the clinician can notice, accept, and utilize according to the "As you experience this, you can experience that" chaining formula. The client need not close his or her eyes in order to experience hypnosis, but the clinician may want to suggest eye closure by offering a direct or indirect suggestion to do so.

In the approach building on formal experience with hypnosis, the typical preinduction phase can focus the client's attention on the range of possibilities hypnosis allows and on how previous experience with hypnosis can make future experiences more satisfying and successful. It seems worthwhile to reiterate a point made in an earlier chapter about exploring the nature and quality of the client's previous hypnotic experience(s). If the client has had a positive and meaningful experience with hypnosis, then the clinician has a solid base on which to build. If the client has had a negative experience with hypnosis (i.e., one that was unsuccessful at least or hurtful at most), then the clinician must exercise caution and refer back to that experience as little as possible in the course of doing hypnosis. Questioning about techniques used and identifying the situational and interpersonal variables operating at the time can save you from unwittingly duplicating a previously negative experience.

If the client has had a positive experience with hypnosis before, a content-filled approach to the use of the formal hypnotic experience can involve engaging the client in an ever-slowing, detailed account of that experience. This approach usually involves a large degree of interaction as the induction progresses, with the clinician simultaneously questioning the client, suggesting possible responses, and building on the client's responses as they occur. The mechanism of induction is structurally the same as in using informal previous hypnotic experiences: As the person becomes absorbed in the memory, the responses associated with that memory grow more pronounced in the here-and-now. The clinician notices, accepts, and utilizes those responses, building toward the goal of the interaction.

Making use of the client's previous experiences with hypnosis, whether formal or informal, is one of the easiest yet most effective induction and deepening processes. It is a spontaneous, loosely structured approach that generates little resistance because "we're not talking about *now*, we're talking about *then*." The extra psychological distance makes a difference. In sum, the techniques involving use of past hypnotic experiences are reliable and flexible ones, and, when well practiced, can comprise a significant portion of your induction repertoire (Grinder & Bandler, 1981; Zeig, 1988).

Building an Internal Focus

The induction process of building an internal focus involves offering *pacing statements* of what external stimuli the client can now be aware of, *coupled with leading statements* describing internal responses the client may come to experience. This can be done in any ratio of pacing to leading statements judged to be useful. In other words, the number of externally oriented suggestions of experience you offer for every internally oriented suggestion of experience is dependent solely on the responsiveness of your client.

Once the assessment is made about how internally or externally focused the client is at the time you would like to begin your induction, you can make the judgment of what ratio of external paces to internal leads you think would be effective, modifying it as necessary according to your client's response. Some clients are so internally focused at the beginning point that you don't have to do much of an induction beyond, "You can go into hypnosis, now." Others may be so externally focused that they may require five or even 10 external paces before a single internal lead is offered. As the induction progresses, fewer and fewer externally oriented statements are made while more and more internally oriented suggestions are offered.

Which externals and which internals you use in what combination in which modality and in which style and structure make for a huge range of possibilities (Grinder & Bandler, 1981).

Metaphorical Inductions with Embedded Suggestions

Rather than use the client's personal past experience as the basis for induction, you can employ metaphors that describe some other person's (or animal's, or thing's) experience at some other time in some other place. Thus, the degree of removal is even greater and thus the possibility for personal threat reduced even further.

The specific dynamics of meaningful metaphor construction could fill volumes, and so can only be superficially presented in this book. When you formulate a metaphor for the induction of hypnosis, it is helpful to know something of the client's personal interests, values, and hobbies. Metaphors built around things that are already a part of the client's lifestyle are more likely to capture and maintain his or her interest. Of course, things of an intrinsically fascinating nature will also do. The broader the base of knowledge and experience a clinician has, the more sophisticated his or her metaphors can be. Metaphor as an induction method can introduce the client to other clients' experiences, build a rapport with the clinician, build an identification with the character(s) of the story, and confuse the client as to why the story is being told. This stimulates a search for meaning and relevance, all the while building an internal focus and receptivity for the subsequent intervention (Barker, 1985; Brown, 1993; Eisen, 1993; Hammond, 1990; Lankton & Lankton, 1989; Mills & Crowley, 1988).

Induction Through Negative Suggestion

In those clients where control is a critical personal issue, a tendency to respond negatively or in a contrary manner is frequently evident. If the clinician says, "It's day," the client responding in a polar response style disagrees and says, "It's night."

In the hypnotic interaction, the negative response style can be accepted and utilized in the service of induction and utilization. The principle underlying the use of negative suggestions is "fight fire with fire." When negative suggestions are offered to the critical, controlling client, he or she can naturally reject them and respond in an opposite way. Knowing the client's tendency to respond in such a manner, the clinician can use negative suggestions the client will reject in order to get the opposite response(s) actually desired. Beware, though, for offering such negative suggestions will seem an obvious trick unless they are offered in a very congruent and meaningful manner.

The use of negative suggestions in the induction phase of hypnotic interaction is intended to use a client's resistance to help him or her into hypnosis. At some point, the client realizes that all your suggestions about *not* relaxing, *not* letting go, *not* focusing internally, etc., have had the effect of facilitating the attainment of hypnosis. This can be, and usually is, a turning point in the relationship. The client has now had his or her experience guided by the clinician, and not only survived it but actually found it pleasant and relaxing. The relief that comes from not having to fight to maintain control can have a profound impact on the client, who has now learned from the experience that he or she can still be in control without having to fight others off negatively. This experience can then serve as a basis for future hypnotic experiences conducted in a more positive framework (Grinder & Bandler, 1981; Erickson & Rossi, 1979; Johnson, 1988).

Induction Through Confusion Techniques

Confusion techniques are among the most complex hypnotic patterns to master because they are, well, confusing. Confusion techniques deliberately disrupt the client's everyday mental set in order to increase the likelihood of a suggestion getting in.

When people are confused, they STOP! And then they develop an internal focus (a self-induced hypnotic state) as they quickly sort through everything they know in order to resolve the confusion. While the person's conscious mind is so preoccupied with making sense of something, the unconscious is more readily available for suggestion.

Confusion techniques can take a variety of forms, but generally fall into one of two categories: pattern interruption techniques and overload techniques. Pattern interruption techniques involve saying and/or doing something to interrupt the person's routine response style in a given area.

Sensory overload involves so overloading the person's conscious mind with information coming in from multiple sources that it can't possibly keep up; thus, the unconscious is engaged to a greater degree.

Confusion techniques for the purpose of induction require a clear-headedness on the part of the clinician, who must know what he or she is doing at each moment. It also requires some dissociation on the part of the clinician in order not to get caught up in the confusion he or she is creating (Erickson, 1964; Gilligan 1987; Otani, 1989b).

CONCLUSION

The approaches presented in this chapter are among the most spontaneous and effective means for inducing hypnotic states in a naturalistic way. Their inability to be scripted in a word-for-word manner is actually their strength. Clinicians who develop skill in the use of these approaches will have done so only through multiple sessions of practicing careful observation of client responses while developing the flexibility to turn each obtained response into one that enhances the quality of the interaction.

REFERENCES

Barker, P. (1985). *Using metaphors in psychotherapy.* New York: Brunner/Mazel.

Brown, P. (1993). Hypnosis and metaphor. In J. Rhue, S. Lynn & I. Kirsch (Eds.), *Handbook of clinical hypnosis* (pp. 291–308). Washington, DC: American Psychological Association.

Eisen, M. (1993). Psychoanalytic and psychodynamic models of hypnoanalysis. In J. Rhue, S. Lynn & I. Kirsch (Eds.), *Handbook of clinical hypnosis* (pp. 123–149). Washington, DC: American Psychological Association.

Erickson, M. (1958). Naturalistic techniques of hypnosis. *American Journal of Clinical Hypnosis, 1,* 3–8.

Erickson, M. (1964). The confusion technique in hypnosis. *American Journal of Clinical Hypnosis, 6,* 185–207.

Erickson, M. & Rossi, E. (1979). *Hypnotherapy: An exploratory casebook.* New York: Irvington.

Gilligan, S. (1987). *Therapeutic trances: The cooperation principle in Ericksonian hypnotherapy.* New York: Brunner/Mazel.

Grinder, J. & Bandler, R. (1981). *Trance-formations: Neuro-Linguistic Programming and the structure of hypnosis.* Moab, UT: Real People Press.

Haley, J. (1973). *Uncommon therapy.* New York: Norton.

Hammond, D. (Ed.) (1990). *Handbook of hypnotic suggestions and metaphors.* New York: Norton.

Johnson, L. (1988). Naturalistic techniques with the "difficult" patient. In J. Zeig & S. Lankton (Eds.), *Developing Ericksonian therapy: State of the art* (pp. 397–413). New York: Brunner/Mazel.

Lankton, C. & Lankton, S. (1989). *Tales of enchantment: Goal-oriented metaphors for adults and children in therapy.* New York: Brunner/Mazel.

Lynn, S., Neufeld,V. & Matyi, C. (1987). Inductions versus suggestions: Effects of direct and indirect wording on hypnotic responding and experience. *Journal of Abnormal Psychology, 96,* 76–79.

Mills, J. & Crowley, R. (1988). *Therapeutic metaphors for children and the child within.* New York: Brunner/Mazel.

O'Hanlon, W. (1987). *Taproots.* New York: Norton.

Otani, A. (1989a). An empirical investigation of Milton H. Erickson's approach to trance induction: A Mark or chain analysis of two published cases. In S. Lankton (Ed.), *Ericksonian hypnosis: Application, preparation and research* (pp. 55–68). New York: Brunner/Mazel.

Otanti, A. (1989b). The confusion technique untangled: Its theoretical rationale and preliminary classification. *American Journal of Clinical Hypnosis, 31,* 164–172.

Zeig, J. (1988). An Ericksonian phenomenological approach to therapeutic hypnotic induction and symptom utilization. In J. Zeig & S. Lankton (Eds.), *Developing Ericksonian therapy: State of the art* (pp. 353–375). New York: Brunner/Mazel.

Zeig, J. & Rennick, P. (1991). Ericksonian hypnotherapy: A communications approach to hypnosis. In S. Lynn & J. Rhue (Eds.), *Theories of hypnosis: Current models and perspectives* (pp. 275–300). New York: Guilford.

17

HYPNOTIC PHENOMENA
AND THEIR INDUCTIONS

Various classical hypnotic phenomena that will be described and defined in this chapter are the basic ingredients for the therapeutic applications of hypnosis. Furthermore, they are the basic building blocks for *all* experience; the structures of hypnosis can be brought together in ways that help or hurt, depending on their associated content.

Here, then are the classical hypnotic phenomena presented in alphabetical order for easy reference.

AGE REGRESSION

Description

Age regression is an intense experiential utilization of memory. Age regression techniques involve either taking the client back in time to some experience in order to reexperience it (called "revivification") as if it were happening in the here-and-now, or simply having the person remember the experience as intensely as possible (called "hypermnesia"). In revivification, the client is immersed in the experience, reliving it exactly as the memory was incorporated at the time it actually happened. In hypermnesia, the person is in the present while simultaneously recalling vividly the details of the memory (Edgette & Edgette, 1995).

Age regression as a category of techniques provides the opportunity to go back in time, whether it be into the recent or distant past, in order to recover forgotten or repressed memories of significant events or to "work through" old memories in order to reach new conclusions (Spiegel, 1993; Weitzenhoffer, 1989).

Strategies of Age Regression

In using age regression clinically, at least two general strategies can be employed, each giving rise to a variety of techniques. The first general strategy concerns the use of age regression to go back to negative, traumatic kinds of experiences. The intention is to allow the client to release pent-up feelings while simultaneously providing new ways of looking at that situation that may help him or her release whatever destructive influences from that experience may still be lingering in his or her life. In this strategy, either revivification or hypermnesia may be employed, depending on the clinician's judgment as to how immersed in or distant from the experience the client can be in order to receive maximum benefit.

The second general strategy of age regression is compatible with and easily integrated with the first. The strategy involves making use of a client's abilities and resources that have been demonstrated in past situations but are not currently being used, unfortunately to his or her own detriment. Often, clients have abilities they don't realize they have, and because they don't have awareness of them and access to them, these abilities lie dormant. In using age regression, the clinician can help clients rediscover in their own past personal experience the very abilities that will allow them to manage current difficulties in a more adaptive way (Edelstein, 1986; Lankton & Lankton, 1983).

Approaches

Any pattern of communication that helps the client go back in time is an approach to age regression. One set of patterns of age regression employs suggestions that involve the use of one's imagination as the trigger to recapture past experiences. Others involve more naturalistic, everyday approaches to immersion in memory. Either approach can be a good one, depending on the client.

Patterns that make use of the client's imagination include the various "special vehicle" approaches (i.e., train, plane, time machine, space ship, elevator, and the like) that can transport the client back in time to the event under consideration. The special vehicle is an artificial, concrete, and content-oriented means for structuring the experience, and thus requires a considerable amount of detail in order to facilitate the regressive process for the client.

More naturalistic approaches to age regression involve offering indirect suggestions to become engaged in memory without the formality of saying, "Now you can go back in the past." Patterns include asking experiential questions to orient the person to his or her own past personal history, and sharing learnings from personal or professional experiences (e.g., "Can you recall how good you felt when you graduated?"). Asking questions to orient the person to his or her own past experiences as an approach involves the client in a search through the past in order to recall the appropriate events necessary to respond meaningfully. Such a search can start out as a more distant memory simply being cognitively remembered, but then skillful further questioning can begin to immerse the client in the memory in order to actually reexperience it.

In order to make the experience of going back into the past less personally threatening, the clinician can indirectly facilitate regression by describing his or her own relevant past learnings, or the relevant past learnings of others. When the experience of others is described, the client naturally tends to project himself or herself into the presented situation, imagining how he or she would feel or act in that situation. Talking about the experience of others as children, for example, can build an identification for the client on the basis of his or her own experiences as a child. Thus, the regression occurs indirectly through identification and projection, and the client can go back in time to recall or reexperience the relevant memories (Erickson & Rossi, 1979).

Other techniques for age regression include: 1) affect or somatic bridging, where the client's current feeling or awareness is linked ("bridged") to the first or one of the first times he or she had that same feeling or awareness ("... and as you continue to be aware of that 'abandoned feeling' you've described, you can drift back in time and recall the first time you ever had that same feeling"); 2) temporal disorientation, in which confusional suggestions are employed to disorient the client from "now" and reorient the person to "then" ("What happens now and then is that remembering then now reminds you now of then when then is so important and when then becomes now because yesterday led to today and you can remember yesterday as if it were now because now and then remembering then as if it were now can be so important..."); and 3) age progression and regression in which the client is first guided into the future at which time he or she can remember the things that have happened in her past ("Look forward to the times that you can look back..."). By orienting to the future first, even greater emotional distance is created from past experiences, making them easier to recapture and use therapeutically (Erickson, 1954; Gilligan, 1987; Hammond, 1990; Watkins, 1971).

AGE PROGRESSION

Description

Age progression involves a utilization of projections of the future. Age progression involves "guiding" the client into the future, where he or she may have the opportunity to imagine the consequences of current changes or experiences, integrate meanings at deeper levels, and, in general, obtain more of an overview of his or her life than day-to-day living typically affords. You can think of it as encouraging hindsight while it is still foresight.

Age progression can be used in at least two general, complementary ways. One is as a check on your work, and the other is as a therapeutic intervention. Both applications involve guiding the client into a future orientation, but for different purposes.

Utilizing an age progression for the purpose of checking on your work is one way of assessing two very important dimensions of therapeutic intervention. Specifically, you can assess whether the intervention's results will be lasting ones and what impact on the client's life system the intervention may ultimately have (Erickson, 1954; Havens, 1986; Phillips & Frederick, 1992).

Approaches

The direct approaches for facilitating age progression relate closely to the direct approaches described for age regression: a "special vehicle" to go into the future, a movie screen on which to watch a movie of the future, a book in which to read about the future, and a collection of photographs of future events are all structured approaches to facilitate a future orientation or projection.

Indirect suggestions for future orientation may include: 1) metaphorical approaches ("I'd like to tell you about a client I worked with who could clearly imagine herself two months after our session doing exactly what we're talking about now and when she saw herself that way she discovered ..."); 2) embedded commands ("I sometimes like to look around and wonder what will happen in the future when you can look back at and feel good about all the changes you have made..."); 3) presuppositions ("I wonder exactly where you will be and what you'll be doing when you happily realize you haven't smoked in days..."); and 4) indirect embedded questions ("You can tell me about how you will describe the way you solved this problem to your friends, can't you?"). Each of these approaches and examples demonstrates a capacity for guiding the client into a mental set for developing positive expectations for the future (deShazer, 1978; Hammond, 1990; Lazarus, 1984; Torem, 1992; Yapko, 1988, 1992).

AMNESIA

Description

Amnesia is a loss of memory; it can be most simply described as the experience of forgetting something. The classic defense mechanism called "repression" is the primary mechanism of hypnotic or structured amnesia.

By inducing the client to consciously forget the various suggestions and experiences provided, you can enable the client's unconscious to form its own unique response, free to use the hypnotic experience as creatively and idiosyncratically as desired.

Beyond offering therapeutic suggestions to the unconscious mind for it to do with as it sees fit, one can use amnesia more directly and purposefully to repress hurtful memories. Suggestions for amnesia in such cases are likely to be accepted only when some healing (i.e., resolution, catharsis) has occurred first.

Amnesia is *not* automatic with hypnosis, as many erroneously believe. If a client is motivated to remember suggestions and experiences, he or she will (Erickson & Rossi, 1974; Zeig, 1985).

Approaches

Amnesia, more so than any of the other various hypnotic phenomena, is less likely to be obtained the more directly you suggest it. Suggesting to someone that he or she "forget everything that took place during this time" can be very threatening on some levels, even to a responsive and obedient client. Thus, in facilitating amnesia in a client, indirect approaches are much more palatable to people, in my experience.

If a direct approach to amnesia is employed, it is probably more likely to be accepted if offered in a more permissive manner. Indirect approaches may take a variety of forms, including indirect suggestions, attentional shifts, and confusion (Cooper, 1979; Evans, 1986; Hilgard, 1968; Zeig, 1985).

ANALGESIA AND ANESTHESIA

Description

Hypnotically induced analgesia and anesthesia are on a continuum of diminishing bodily sensation. Analgesia refers to a reduction in the sensation of pain, allowing associated sensations (e.g., pressure, temperature, position) that orient the client to his or her body to remain. Anesthesia refers to a complete or near complete elimination of sensation in all or part of the body.

The potential to reduce pain to a manageable level is a genuine tribute to the capabilities of the human mind, and constitutes one of the most meaningful applications of therapeutic hypnosis. Working with clients in pain requires a very broad base of understanding of hypnotic principles, human physiology, psychological motivations, human information processing, and interpersonal dynamics. Clients in pain are in some ways easy to work with because of their (usually) high level of motivation, and yet in other ways such clients are exceptionally difficult to work with because of the impact of the pain on all levels of their lives. Therefore, approaching the person in pain must be done sensitively, with an appreciation that the pain is often more than pain: It can be a source of anxiety, feelings of helplessness and depression, increased dependency, and restricted social contact.

Even pain emanating from clearly organic causes has psychological components to it, particularly how the suffering person experiences the pain and its consequences. It is the psychological dimension of the pain that is most overtly affected by hypnosis for a variety of reasons that all seem to stem from the greater self-mastery hypnosis affords. Fear and anxiety, feelings of helplessness, and negative expectations can all be reduced with the use of hypnosis. The physical components of the pain are also addressed by the use of hypnosis, evidenced in the various healing strategies employing hypnotic patterns.

Using hypnosis in the management of pain is advantageous for some very important reasons. First, and foremost, in my opinion, is the opportunity for greater self-control and, therefore, greater personal responsibility for one's level of well-being. Feeling victimized, whether by pain or by other people, puts one in a helpless position from which it is difficult to do any real healing. Having self control is extremely important to the person in pain, and hypnosis facilitates its acquisition.

Second, because the ability to experience hypnosis is a natural one existing within the person, pain medications may be reduced or even eliminated. Hypnosis has no side effects, nor is it addictive. The pain is reduced in differing degrees in different people, but whatever the result, it is obtained safely and naturally.

Third, hypnosis permits a higher level of functioning and enhances the healing process in persons who utilize hypnotic patterns. Remaining as active as your condition allows is important on all levels, and can make a significant difference in the problem's course. The expectation of wellness, the experience of comfort, and the diminished anxiety and fear can all be important factors in facilitating recovery, at most, or retarding decline, at least (Brown & Fromm, 1986, 1987; Chaves, 1989, 1993; Crasilneck & Hall, 1985).

Approaches

Analgesia often arises spontaneously during hypnosis for the client who is sufficiently absorbed in the experience. Associated with the inhibition of voluntary movement (catalepsy) that is evident in the hypnotized person is a diminished awareness for one's body, hence the analgesia. Therefore, any approach that successfully shifts the person's awareness away from the bodily sensation(s) under consideration can have an indirect analgesic effect. With training and reinforcing practice sessions, the client in pain can learn to distract himself or herself, and then refocus on positive ideas, feelings, memories, or whatever he or she chooses as a focal point. The teaching of self-hypnosis is essential in order for this approach to the management of pain to work (see Chapter 18).

Direct suggestions of analgesia as an approach involves offering suggestions for the reduction or lack of sensation in the specific part of the client that is painful. Another direct approach, though slightly less so, is the "glove anesthesia." In this sensory alteration process, the client is given suggestions to experience anesthesia in either or both hands. When the suggested anesthesia has been accomplished, further suggestions may be given that the anesthesia can be effectively transferred to whatever part of the body he or she chooses.

Physical dissociation as an approach to facilitating analgesia can involve guiding clients into the subjective experience that their mind and body are existing on two different and separate levels of experience. There can be sufficient distance between them for the client not to notice what his or her body is experiencing.

Other approaches to analgesia include: 1) amnesia, in which the client is offered suggestions to forget having had pain. This interrupts the experience of the pain being continuous, and thus paves the way for intermittent and increasing periods of comfort as far as the client can remember; 2) gradual diminution, in which suggestions are offered that the discomfort decreases slowly over some specific span of time; 3) pseudo-orientation in time, in which the client is age-progressed to a time of post-recovery; 4) time distortion, in which moments of comfort can be expanded in subjective perception (see the later section in this chapter on time distortion); and 5) regression, in which the person is age-regressed back to a time period prior to the pain's onset (Barber, 1977; Barber & Adrian, 1982; Erickson, 1966; Erickson, 1983; Hammond, 1990; Hilgard & Hilgard, 1994).

CATALEPSY

Description

Catalepsy is defined as the inhibition of voluntary movement associated with the intense focusing on a specific stimulus. The degree to which the client is focused on the associations triggered by the clinician is the degree to which the client can demonstrate cataleptic responses. Such responses may include a fixed gaze, general immobility, the "waxy flexibility" usually associated with the catatonic patient who maintains his or her limbs in whatever position the clinician places them, muscular rigidity, unconscious movements, and the slowing of basic physical processes such as breathing, blinking, and swallowing. Signs of catalepsy can be relied on to a large extent as indicators of hypnosis (both formally induced and spontaneous) or they may be suggested for specific therapeutic reasons to be described shortly.

Catalepsy must be considered one of the most basic features of hypnosis, for it is associated directly or indirectly with virtually every other hypnotic phenomenon. Catalepsy is the result of focusing on a new and different reality, whatever it may be, and thus paves the way to let go of the "old" reality long enough to create a therapeutic experience of age regression, analgesia, sensory distortions, or whatever.

Catalepsy implies an intense engagement on one or more levels that indicates a high degree of activity and receptiveness to the guidance of the clinician on other levels. This is why a client focused on one level may have his arm placed in a position and leave it there, literally too preoccupied with other things to think to move it.

Therapeutic purposes for obtaining catalepsy as a response are numerous, but can be described in two general ways. Catalepsy can either be a target response in and of itself or it can serve to facilitate further hypnotic involvement through the client's recognition of his or her own unconscious mind's ability to respond in automatic ways. Catalepsy as a target response may be used, for example, to assist any patient whose movements must be minimal in order for him or her to recover more quickly and comfortably. As a facilitator of further hypnotic experience, catalepsy can be a basis for securing and maintaining attention (thus an inducer), facilitating greater independent activity of the unconscious mind and increasing the degree of involvement or focus of the client (thus a deepener) (Erickson & Rossi, 1976, 1979; Weitzenhoffer, 1989).

Approaches

Anything that captures the intense interest of the client can facilitate cataleptic responses, including interesting stories, surprises or shocks, and confusion (Bloom, 1990; Rossi, 1973). Obtaining catalepsy as a response from the client can be accomplished directly or indirectly, verbally or nonverbally, as desired. The most common way to encourage catalepsy is to simply offer general suggestions for relaxation and immobility.

Probably the best and most practical example of facilitating hypnosis or catalepsy through a nonverbal means of suggestion is the indirect technique of modeling. Using your body as a model, you can deliberately shift from the animated patterns of routine conversation to a demonstration to your client of the potential immobility of the hypnotic state (Erickson, 1983, 1985; Gilligan, 1987).

DISSOCIATION

Description

Dissociation is defined as the ability to break a global experience into its component parts, amplifying awareness for one part while diminishing awareness for the others. Unfortunately, most therapists seem to only know about dissociation in its pathological forms, and never learn how to facilitate its therapeutic applications.

Through dissociation, people do not have to be attached to their immediate experience, involved and "present." They can "go through the motions," but not really be "there." The conscious mind can drift off somewhere, preoccupied with whatever else has its attention, and therefore the unconscious is free to respond in whatever way it chooses. Thus, the deeper the hypnotic state, the greater the degree of dissociation and the greater the opportunity for unconscious responses.

Hypnosis necessarily involves dissociation, which is the reason dissociation was also discussed earlier as a basic hypnotic characteristic. Dissociation allows for the automatic, or spontaneous, responses of the client to occur; the repressed or forgotten memory can be remembered, the hand can lift unconsciously, the body can forget to move or notice sensation, and so forth (Cardena & Spiegel, 1991; Hilgard, 1986; Spiegel, 1993).

Approaches

Suggestions that facilitate divisions of experience are suggestions for dissociation. For example, each of the hypnotic inductions described earlier will generate a conscious-unconscious dissociation through its emphasis on the client's ability to experience things and learn things effortlessly and automatically. The conscious mind is given ideas and experiences to focus on while the unconscious is encouraged to respond in other ways and learn at levels outside of awareness.

Direct suggestions for division let the client discover (or rediscover, as the case may be) that it is possible to have experiences on different levels, and that these experiences can occur spontaneously, automatically, and with no deliberate planning.

Dissociation is indirectly suggested whenever suggestions for a particular hypnotic phenomenon are offered. Use of metaphors, confusion, and other forms of indirect suggestion all may facilitate dissociation (Bandler & Grinder, 1979; Gilligan, 1987; Grinder & Bandler, 1981; Hammond, 1990; Watkins & Watkins, 1993).

HALLUCINATIONS AND SENSORY ALTERATIONS

Description

Hallucinations created hypnotically are suggested experiences the client can have that are clearly removed from current, more objective realities.

A hallucination is, by definition, a sensory experience that does *not* arise from external stimulation. Hallucinations can be characterized as being either "positive" or "negative." These terms do *not* refer to the emotional impact of the hallucination(s) on the person experiencing it. Rather, these terms refer to the structure of the hallucinations.

A positive hallucination is defined as having the (visual, auditory, kinesthetic, olfactory, gustatory) experience of something that is not objectively present. A negative hallucination is *not* experiencing something sensorily that *is* objectively present (it is the flip side of the positive hallucination).

In facilitating hallucinations, the clinician is altering awareness for sensory input. Guiding clients into situations where they can experience themselves or the world differently obviously increases the range of their experiences and can thus instill valuable new resources (Bandler & Grinder, 1979; Hilgard, 1986; Weitzenhoffer, 1989).

Approaches

Hallucinations can and often do arise spontaneously. To deliberately facilitate the experience of hallucinations, both direct and indirect approaches can work well.

A direct suggestion to experience something is often sufficient; usually, by the time the clinician attempts to facilitate hallucinations, the rapport and responsiveness are already accomplished.

Suggestions for hallucinations, whether positive or negative, should generally be offered in a positive suggestion structure so the clients know what they should experience, and not what they shouldn't.

Indirect suggestions may also be used to facilitate hallucinations. Suggesting that the client be aware of his or her arm is an indirect suggestion not to notice his or her leg (Bandler & Grinder, 1979; Erickson, Rossi & Rossi, 1976; Spanos & Coe, 1992; Young, Bentall, Slade & Dewey, 1987).

IDEODYNAMIC RESPONSES

Description

The automatic functions that humans are capable of exist on at least three different levels: motoric, sensory, and affective. Collectively, these are called the "ideodynamic responses," meaning "conversion of an idea to a dynamic." Individually, the responses are called the "ideomotor response," the "ideosensory response," and the "ideoaffective response." Each is an automatic response generated at an unconscious level in response to a stimulus, either external or internal.

The ideomotor response is the physical manifestation of mental experience, or, in other words, the body's unconscious reactions to your thoughts.

Ideosensory responses are automatic experiences of sensation associated with the processing of suggestions. Having the normal range of sensation and a kinesthetic memory for what the experience of the sensation was is the basis for the ideosensory response.

Ideoaffective responses are the automatic emotional responses attached to the various experiences each person has. It is difficult, if not impossible, to feel entirely neutral about something. Therefore, as the client experiences the suggestions of the clinician, different feelings associated with the ideas contained in the suggestions will inevitably come to the surface.

In doing hypnosis, the ideodynamics are important variables for two important reasons. First, they reflect the inner experience of the client at the levels where change is sought. Second, they are a part of the current therapeutic experience, and will be the action, feeling, and sensory-based components of the therapy that the person will rely on as the basis for change in the future (Cheek, 1994; Erickson & Rossi, 1979, 1981; Gilligan, 1988; Lankton & Lankton, 1983; Weitzenhoffer, 1989).

Approaches

Unlike many of the other hypnotic phenomena, the ideodynamics will occur no matter what you do. There is virtually no way the client can prevent unconscious body movements, or keep from reexperiencing feelings and sensations associated with things you talk about. In facilitating the ideodynamic responses hypnotically, the issue becomes one of whether or not the client responds well to suggestions for specific automatic responses.

Preoccupying the client with the content of the suggestion facilitates the ideodynamic responses, for while the client projects himself or herself into the described situation and attempts to make meaning of it, his or her unconscious is already responding (Erickson & Rossi, 1981; Gilligan, 1987).

TIME DISTORTION

Description

The experience of time is a purely subjective one, meaning you experience the passing of time in your own way at any given moment. The passing of time can seem much longer or much shorter than is objectively true, depending on your focus of attention. Such distortions of time take place in the "everyday hypnosis" all people experience; and, like all experiences that are subjective, the experience of time can be significantly altered in deliberate ways hypnotically (Cooper, 1952; Cooper & Erickson, 1982; Erickson & Erickson, 1958; Zeig, 1980).

Approaches

Approaches for facilitating time distortion can range from "simply getting out of the way" and letting time distortion arise spontaneously to the offering of direct and indirect suggestions for its evolution. Time distortion tends to arise with no suggestions for it at all, for once someone closes his or her eyes and becomes absorbed in internal experience (e.g., thoughts, memories, sensations, etc.), the outside world is in the background and the chance to make a realistic assessment of how much clock time has elapsed is more difficult.

Direct suggestion for time distortion, especially offered permissively, can facilitate the experience well.

Indirect suggestions for time distortion gently plant the notion that the experience of time can be altered. Indirect suggestions, stories containing examples of experiences where time was distorted, conversational postulates, and double binds are all capable of facilitating time distortion (Alman & Lambrou, 1992; Erickson & Erickson, 1958; Hammond, 1990; Lankton & Lankton, 1983; Spiegel & Spiegel, 1987).

ENDING THE HYPNOTIC STATE (DISENGAGEMENT)

As good as it feels to be in hypnosis, eventually you have to disengage from the hypnotic state. Disengagement is the final stage of hypnotic interaction. The client may indicate a readiness to disengage through a diminished focus of his or her attention and by beginning to move and even stretch. The clinician has to make a decision at the moment of observing such signs as to whether the work is done for that session or whether the client's initiation of disengagement is some form of avoidance that may need to be addressed therapeutically.

When and how to disengage is a matter of individual clinical judgment, based on the overall treatment plan and the accomplishments of that specific session.

Most direct approaches to disengagement (traditionally called "awakening") have employed a counting method: "I'm going to count to three and snap my fingers and you will then be wide awake..." Such an approach is not particularly respectful of the client's need to disengage from the hypnotic state at his or her own rate. Expecting a client to respond to an arbitrary count and come out of hypnosis simply because the clinician wants this to happen does not allow the individual whatever time he or she may want to complete the experience comfortably.

If the hypnotic state has been an informal, spontaneous one, the clinician can choose to be consistent in his or her approach by offering indirect suggestions for disengagement.

How the hypnotic experience is concluded will have a significant impact on the client, since human memory is generally strongest for the most recent events (the "recency effect"). In other words, the feeling clients have as they disengage from hypnosis are the feelings they are most likely to associate with the hypnotic experience. Letting clients disengage at their own rate allows them the opportunity to feel relaxed and unhurried under the clinician's care (Erickson & Rossi, 1981; Kirsch, Lynn & Rhue, 1993; Watkins, 1986).

CONCLUSION

Clinical interventions will always involve some or all of the classical hypnotic phenomena. Therefore, it is imperative that you be clear about what each of these subjective experiences that individuals are capable of really is. Before you can apply them in the meaningful ways described, it is most helpful to observe these experiences as they arise in daily living, attempting to uncover what stimulus in the observed event acted as the trigger for the hypnotic phenomenon.

REFERENCES

Alman, B. & Lambrou, P. (1992). *Self-hypnosis: The complete manual for health and self-change.* New York: Brunner/Mazel.

Bandler, R. & Grinder, J. (1979). *Frogs into princes.* Moab, UT: Real People Press.

Barber, J. (1977). Rapid induction analgesia: A clinical report. *American Journal of Clinical Hypnosis, 19*, 138–149.

Barber, J. & Adrian, C. (Eds.) (1982). *Psychological approaches to the management of pain.* New York: Brunner/Mazel.

Bloom, P. (1990). The creative process in hypnotherapy. In M. Fass & D. Brown (Eds.), *Creative mastery in hypnosis and hypnoanalysis: A festschrift for Erika Fromm.* Hillsdale, NJ: Erlbaum.

Brown, D. & Fromm, E. (1986). *Hypnotherapy and hypnoanalysis.* Hillsdale, NJ: Erlbaum.

Brown, D. & Fromm, E. (1987). *Hypnosis and behavioral medicine.* Hillsdale, NJ: Erlbaum.

Cardena, E. & Spiegel, D. (1991). Suggestibility, absorption, and dissociation: An integrative model of hypnosis. In J. Schumaker (Ed.), *Human suggestibility: Advances in theory, research, and application* (pp. 93–107). New York: Routledge & Kegan Paul.

Chaves, J. (1989). Hypnotic control of clinical pain. In N. Spanos & J.Chaves (Eds.), *Hypnosis: The cognitive-behavioral perspective.* Buffalo, NY: Prometheus Books.

Chaves, J. (1993). Hypnosis in pain management. In J. Rhue, S. Lynn & I. Kirsch (Eds.), *Handbook of clinical hypnosis* (pp. 511–532). Washington, DC: American Psychological Association.

Cheek, D. (1994). *Hypnosis: The application of ideomotor techniques.* Boston, MA: Allyn & Bacon.

Cooper, L. (1952). Time distortion in hypnosis. *Journal of Psychology, 34*, 247–284.

Cooper, L. (1979). Hypnotic amnesia. In E. Fromm & R. Shor (Eds.), *Hypnosis: Developments in research and new perspectives* (pp. 305–351). New York: Aldine Atherton.

Cooper, L. & Erickson, M. (1959; 1982). *Time distortion in hypnosis: An experimental and clinical investigation* (2nd. ed.). New York: Irvington.

Crasilneck, H. & Hall, J. (1985). *Clinical hypnosis: Principles and applications.* Orlando: Grune & Stratton.

deShazer, S. (1978). Brief hypnotherapy of two sexual dysfunctions: The crystal ball technique. *American Journal of Clinical Hypnosis, 20,* 203–208.

Edelstein, M. (1986). Age regression. In B. Zilbergeld, M. Edelstein & D. Araoz (Eds.), *Hypnosis: Questions and answers* (pp. 155–159). New York: Norton.

Edgette, J. H. & Edgette, J. S. (1995). *The handbook of hypnotic phenomena in psychotherapy.* New York: Brunner/Mazel

Erickson, M. (1954). Pseudo-orientation in time as a hypnotherapeutic procedure. *International Journal of Clinical and Experimental Hypnosis, 2,* 261–283.

Erickson, M. (1966). The interspersal hypnotic technique for symptom correction and pain control. *American Journal of Clinical Hypnosis, 8,* 198–209.

Erickson, M. (1983). *Healing in hypnosis.* E. Rossi, M. Ryan & F. Sharp (Eds.) New York: Irvington.

Erickson, M. (1985). *Life reframing in hypnosis.* E. Rossi & M. Ryan (Eds.). New York: Irvington.

Erickson, M. & Erickson, E. (1958). Further considerations of time distortion: Subjective time condensation as distinct from time expansion. *American Journal of Clinical Hypnosis, 1,* 83–88.

Erickson, M. & Rossi, E. (1974). Varieties of hypnotic amnesia. *American Journal of Clinical Hypnosis, 4,* 225–239.

Erickson, M. & Rossi, E. (1979). *Hypnotherapy: An exploratory casebook.* New York: Irvington.

Erickson, M. & Rossi, E. (1981). *Experiencing hypnosis.* New York: Irvington.

Erickson, M., Rossi, S. & Rossi, E. (1976). *Hypnotic realities.* New York: Irvington.

Evans, F. (1986). The importance and role of posthypnotic amnesia. In B. Zilbergeld, M. Edelstein & D. Araoz (Eds.), *Hypnosis: Questions and answers* (pp. 173–180). New York: Norton.

Gilligan, S. (1987). *Therapeutic trances: The cooperation principle in Ericksonian hypnotherapy.* New York: Brunner/Mazel.

Gilligan, S. (1988). Symptom phenomena as trance phenomena. In. J. Zeig & S. Lankton (Eds.), *Developing Ericksonian therapy: State of the art* (pp. 327–352). New York: Brunner/Mazel.

Grinder, J. & Bandler, R. (1981). *Trance-formations: Neuro-Linguistic Programming and the structure of hypnosis.* Moab, UT: Real People Press.

Hammond, D. (Ed.) (1990). *Handbook of hypnotic suggestions and metaphors.* New York: Norton.

Havens, R. (1986). Posthypnotic predetermination of therapeutic progress. *American Journal of Clinical Hypnosis, 28,* 258–262.

Hilgard, E. (1968). *The experience of hypnosis.* New York: Harcourt Brace Jovanovich.

Hilgard, E. & Hilgard, J. (1994). *Hypnosis in the relief of pain.* New York: Brunner/Mazel.

Hilgard, E. (1986). *Divided consciousness: Multiple controls in human thought and action.* New York: John Wiley & Sons.

Kirsch, I., Lynn, S. & Rhue, J. (1993). Introduction to clinical hypnosis. In J. Rhue, S. Lynn & I. Kirsch (Eds.), *Handbook of clinical hypnosis* (pp. 3–22). Washington, DC: American Psychological Association.

Lankton, S. & Lankton, C. (1983). *The answer within: A clinical framework of Ericksonian hypnotherapy.* New York: Brunner/Mazel.

Lazarus, A. (1984). *In the mind's eye: The power of imagery for personal enrichment.* New York: Guilford.

Nash, M. (1987). What, if anything, is regressed about hypnotic age regression? A review of the empirical literature. *Psychological Bulletin, 102*, 42–52.

Phillips, M. & Frederick, C. (1992). The use of progressions as prognostic, ego-strengthening, and integrating techniques. *American Journal of Clinical Hypnosis, 35*, 99–108.

Rossi, E. (1973). Psychological shocks and creative moments in psychotherapy. *American Journal of Clinical Hypnosis, 16*, 9–22.

Rossi, E. & Cheek, D. (1988). *Mind-body therapy.* New York: Norton.

Spanos, N. & Coe, W. (1992). A social-psychological approach to hypnosis. In E. Fromm & M. Nash (Eds.), *Contemporary hypnosis research* (pp. 102–130). New York: Guilford.

Spiegel, D. (1993). Hypnosis in the treatment of post-traumatic stress disorders. In J. Rhue, S. Lynn & I. Kirsch (Eds.), *Handbook of clinical hypnosis* (pp. 493–508). Washington, DC: American Psychological Association.

Torem, M. (1992). "Back from the future": A powerful age-progression technique. *American Journal of Clinical Hypnosis, 35*, 2, 81–88.

Watkins, J. (1971). The affect bridge: A hypnoanalytic technique. *International Journal of Clinical and Experimental Hypnosis, 19*, 1, 21–27.

Watkins, J. (1986). Handling a patient who doesn't come out of trance. In B. Zilbergeld, M. Edelstein & D. Araoz (Eds.), *Hypnosis: Questions and answers* (pp. 445–447). New York: Norton.

Watkins, J. & Watkins, H. (1993). Accessing the relevant area of personality functioning. *American Journal of Clinical Hypnosis, 35*, 4, 277–284.

Weitzenhoffer, A. (1989). *The practice of hypnotism* (Vol.1). New York: John Wiley & Sons.

Yapko, M. (1988). *When living hurts: Directives for treating depression.* New York: Brunner/Mazel.

Yapko, M. (1992). *Hypnosis and the treatment of depressions.* New York: Brunner/Mazel.

Young, H., Bentall, R., Slade, P. & Dewey, M. (1987). The role of brief instructions and suggestibility in the elicitation of auditory and visual hallucinations in normal and psychiatric subjects. *Journal of Nervous and Mental Disease, 175*, 41–48.

Zeig, J. (Ed.) (1980). *A teaching seminar with Milton H. Erickson, M.D.* New York: Brunner/Mazel.

Zeig, J. (1985). The clinical use of amnesia: Ericksonian methods. In J. Zeig (Ed.), *Ericksonian Psychotherapy: Vol. 1, Structures* (pp. 317–337). New York: Brunner/Mazel.

18

SELF-HYPNOSIS AND THE SELF OF THE THERAPIST

What is your "internal environment" like? Is it comfortable? Stressful? Are you generally self-accepting or are you self-critical? Throughout this book, I have been emphasizing the role of communication— including communication with yourself—in either enhancing or diminishing one's experience.

In some ways, what "psychopathology" is about to a huge extent is the fact that people think hurtful things (about themselves, about others, about life, about *whatever*) and then make the mistake of actually *believing* themselves. So when someone says to himself or herself, "I'll never have a good relationship," if he or she accepts that as true then it can easily become a hurtful self-fulfilling prophecy. Ernest Hilgard, a very important figure in the world of hypnosis, once called hypnosis "believed-in imagination." If people come to believe helpful things they tell themselves ("I can do this, even though I'm a little intimidated by it"), these aren't identified or presented as symptoms. Therapists hear only about the hurtful things people tell themselves—and the associated consequences.

I think it is a shame that therapists tend to focus only on pathology and weakness, rather than on strengths and skills. I think the more you learn about the internal experiences of people who do something well, the more you learns how to correct or refocus those people who are doing badly in that same arena. For example, people who are fearful of public speaking create (typically, through imagery) vivid visual images of themselves standing in front of and speaking to a room full of people (or even just a few others) who seem bored, irritated, and otherwise antagonistic. They visualize themselves in great detail messing up their presentation, and looking foolish in the eyes of everyone present. Then they have all the anxious and terrified feelings (ideoaffective responses) as if those images were real. People who don't have a fear of public speaking don't visualize failure. Lengthy analysis about "why" someone has a fear of public speaking is utterly irrelevant if he or she continues to generate those same hurtful images. No "mop-up" relaxation process can compete with the power of such anxiety-provoking images if they are allowed to continue. Therapy has to interrupt them.

FOCAL POINTS AND THE QUALITY OF YOUR LIFE

So much of what I have described about hypnosis can be summarized succinctly with two words: *focal point.* Where your attention is focused and what aspects of experience you attend to and engage with determine so much of how you respond and, ultimately, how you feel about yourself. Every situation has many possible focal points. For example, in doing hypnosis you can focus your attention on how you feel as you conduct the session, what words you're going to say, and the images in your mind as you describe them. Your focus is, therefore, primarily internal. If that is so, you will not do hypnosis very well. Unless your attention is focused on your client, you will consistently miss the opportunity to observe and utilize spontaneous responses as they arise.

In another example, if someone is preoccupied and self-absorbed with some problem (internal focus) but feels obligated to go to a party, unless he or she can shift focal points and become externally oriented and engage with others, he or she will be viewed as unapproachable (interpreted by others as arrogant, moody, or shy) and get negative feedback as a result. That will *not* be a cheering experience.

In still another example, if I focus on meeting your needs, and rarely on meeting my own, then I become dependent on you for my self-esteem, fearful of being abandoned, and sadly lacking in awareness for myself as a person.

Hypnosis is about shifting focal points. Hypnosis involves directing people, in one way or another, to focus on ideas that can help their circumstances. Hypnosis involves helping people build the "frame of mind" to do whatever it is they are trying to do, connecting them with the resources they need to accomplish their goals. Thus, in order to be a skilled practitioner, you would have to know what focal points would be useful to engage with in order for your client to succeed.

Now, let's extend this idea to *you.* Self-hypnosis means applying all the same principles to yourself. Using the inductions you learn in this book, you can learn to guide yourself into hypnosis. You can learn to direct your attention to aspects of your experience you normally don't pay much attention to. You can talk to yourself, through your thoughts, about *what* you want to accomplish and *how* you are going to accomplish it. You can use imagery to visualize the successful handling of difficult circumstances, establishing an expectancy that your success can go from possible to probable. You can build on the feelings of desire and recall intensely the feelings associated with taking an intelligent risk and succeeding; then you can extend those feelings to the concerns at hand.

How can you go about learning self-hypnosis? The reference section at the end of this chapter contains some excellent sources for further reading on the subject. My recommendation is to begin by making hypnosis tapes for yourself as if you were your own client. Pick an issue to work on, and create a tape with a process on it (Chapter 21 contains an example of a goal-oriented process from beginning to middle to end that you can use as a model) that addresses your concerns. I suggest you begin by making a tape for several reasons. First, who knows how to talk to you better than you do? Second, as you initially begin to practice self-hypnosis, your attention will typically wander. Having the tape as an external guide allows you to let your attention wander and still return to focusing on the tape. With practice, your attention wanders less and less, and you learn to stay "on track" for increasing lengths of time. And, of course, you can end the session any time you want by reorienting yourself to your usual "waking state" and getting on with your day's agenda. Eventually, the tape becomes irrelevant as you evolve the ability to go into and stay in hypnosis without it. Have more and more of your practice sessions without the tape until you can conduct a meaningful session inside your head without any tape at all.

Self-hypnosis allows you to tap into whichever part(s) of yourself will most benefit you in a given situation. It defines your relationship with yourself as cooperative and respectful, rather than internally conflicted and devaluing.

To function well as a person, as well as a therapist, your "internal environment" must be both developed and protected. It is very comforting to know that you can use your hypnotic skills to improve not only the lives of your clients, but yours as well.

SUGGESTED READINGS

Alman, B. & Lambrou, P. (1992). *Self-hypnosis: The complete manual for health and self-change.* New York: Brunner/Mazel.

Fromm, E. & Kahn, S. (1990). *Self-hypnosis: The Chicago paradigm.* New York: Guilford.

Sanders, S. (1991). *Clinical self-hypnosis: The power of words and images.* New York: Guilford.

Simpkins, C. & Simpkins, A. (1991). *Principles of self-hypnosis: Pathways to the unconscious.* New York: Irvington.

Soskis, D. (1986). *Teaching self-hypnosis.* New York: Norton.

19

THERAPEUTIC UTILIZATION OF THE HYPNOTIC STATE

Utilizing the capacity each person has to experience himself or herself differently in deliberate ways to reach a personal goal is the essence of clinical hypnosis. What resources do people have that can be made available to them in useful ways? What frame of mind do they need to be in order to accomplish their goals?

SYMPTOM STRUCTURES AND HYPNOTIC PHENOMENA

I have previously described the classical hypnotic phenomena as the building blocks of experience. In varying combinations and degrees of purity, these phenomena comprise ongoing experience, whether good or bad.

In the context of conducting therapy, having the ability to identify the various hypnotic phenomena associated with a client's symptoms permits you a more rapid and comprehensive understanding of his or her problem. Knowing the series of steps he or she follows internally in creating the symptom(s) permits you the opportunity to choose at what point in the sequence you may introduce an interruption that alters the sequence in some beneficial way.

The dissociative aspect of symptoms is an especially noteworthy point to appreciate. Therapy clients routinely describe how the symptom "just happens," meaning it is not a voluntary response on the part of the individual. In defining therapy as involving pattern interruption and pattern building, as virtually all therapies must do, it is clear that the role of the clinician is to establish new associations to the client's dysfunctional or self-limiting behaviors, thoughts, and feelings. Such associations can best be built through direct experience, such as hypnotic processes, and through experiential approaches, such as task assignments and behavioral prescriptions.

Utilizing hypnotic phenomena as a reference point can be a useful means for understanding symptom structures. When such hypnotic phenomena are evident in the problem structure, a solution can take the form of building new associations through the use of complementary hypnotic phenomena. It may be a useful exercise useful for you to identify which hypnotic phenomena are evident in the type(s) of disorders you tend to treat most frequently (Araoz, 1985; Gilligan, 1987, 1988; Zeig, 1988).

PATTERNS OF INTERVENTION

Applications of hypnosis are as diverse and creative as the number of clinicians who work with it. There is no human problem that can be solved in all people through a "one size fits all" formula. Simple and direct suggestions for a problem's resolution are considered a possible treatment intervention since they can work with a certain relatively small percentage of the population, but the patterns described here are offered in response to the recognition that most people need something more multidimensional. Individualizing treatment is a necessity, and typically that means tailoring general patterns of intervention to the specific needs of the client. This process is akin to learning the rules and vocabulary of a language, but still expressing yourself in your own way. There are, therefore, patterns that range from relatively simple to very complex and subtle. The following are some of the simpler and more common hypnotic patterns for intervening in client problems.

CHANGING PERSONAL HISTORY

Changing personal history as a therapeutic intervention can involve age regression, age progression, catalepsy, dissociation, hallucinations, and time distortion. The strategy is appropriate to use when a client is presenting a problem that has its origins in an earlier life decision that is proving maladaptive. One decision sets up a lifetime of experiences that support it, even if hurtful. For example, if a client had the experience of being abused as a child and made the decision (i.e., formed the generalization) that the world is an abusive place and people are not to be trusted or related to in a positive way, the clinician might take the client back in time to his earliest memories and facilitate the (imaginary) experience for feeling loved, cared for, and protected by others. When the resources of affection and caring are provided and he or she is then guided forward through time while having those missing resources subjectively present through all his or her life experiences, subjective feelings about self and others can change in a healthier direction.

Some people integrate the new suggested experience and treat it as if it were their real history (even swearing to its authenticity). Others are just grateful to have had the experience and accompanying internal changes while recognizing that it was all part of the hypnotic session.

CRITICAL (TRAUMATIC) INCIDENT PROCESS

No one escapes hurtful experiences, and no one is going to get out of this life alive. Cars crash, people die, wars are fought, and on and on. Despite these harsh realities, it is often the "everyday" traumas that can have the most serious impact: the mean kid who made fun of your freckles, the hole in your pants at the most embarrassing moment possible, and the stupid, insensitive comment that should never have been said are all examples of the "everyday trauma" that can have incredible impact on your life. Years later, such traumas may intellectually seem silly and irrational, yet still carry a big emotional wallop. In people who have suffered a trauma of some sort (even if the trauma may seem mild in nature to the clinician, it is the client's feeling that is the gauge of what is traumatic), the traumatic event may be a turning point in the person's life. If it is a turning point for the worse, which not all traumas are, then the critical incident process may be an appropriate treatment strategy.

The critical incident process involve revivification, catalepsy, dissociation, age progression, and hallucinations. This is an emotionally powerful process, intending to first release pent-up emotions associated with a traumatic event ("catharsis") and then reframe (reinterpret) its meaning. If the client has conscious memory for the content of the critical incident, you may simply proceed in a relatively straightforward way. If the traumatic incident has been forgotten or partially repressed, the process is a bit tricky, since the client's unconscious may have protectively chosen to keep the information out of his or her awareness. In such an instance, you can still do a critical incident process, but you must be careful to let the client work at his or her own rate and to never push the client to deal with something directly he or she chooses not to, except as an absolute last resort. Ideomotor questioning can be enormously useful here to help assess whether the client's unconscious is ready, willing, and able to deal with the traumatic experience and/or the consequences in the client's life (Cheek, 1994; Erickson & Kubie, 1941; Feldman, 1985; Spiegel, 1993; Spiegel & Spiegel, 1987; Yapko, 1992).

HOMEWORK ASSIGNMENTS

Many therapeutic approaches make use of "homework," tasks the client is given to carry out between therapy sessions. These are intended to amplify thoughts, feelings, and behaviors that the clinician judges important in the therapy. The homework assignment operates on the level of direct experience, often a more powerful level than the typical verbal therapy addresses. It is hypnotic in the sense that it can be thought of as an experiential metaphor in the treatment process. In other words, if properly presented, it will address the unconscious dynamics of the presenting problem. When the client engages in an activity that will cause him or her to see himself or herself differently while confronting his or her limiting thoughts, feelings, and behaviors, the desired change may be accomplished (Haley, 1973; Lankton, 1988; Madanes, 1981, 1984; Yapko, 1988).

One type of homework assignment might involve asking a client to conduct an experiment in order to test a hurtful belief he or she holds that is not really true but is believed nonetheless. For example, one client I worked with, who happened to be a therapist, had never taken a vacation in over eight years of clinical practice. He feared "something terrible" would happen to his patients if he was away. I pointed out the value of leisure time and the need for his patients to be independent enough to endure his being away for brief periods of time occasionally. He agreed, and was willing to experiment with a short vacation. Weeks ahead of time he informed his patients of his plans, and gave them the names and numbers of two therapists he arranged to be available to them in his absence. He was encouraged to do all he could to assess and predict any problems his patients might realistically encounter, and left believing he had prepared as best he could. To make a long story short, there were no incidents or problems. He felt he could do it again in the future, acknowleding that "I can prepare only so much, and then it's up to my patients."

REFRAMING

The clinical skill involved in reframing is to suspend the client's belief system long enough to have him or her consider an alternate viewpoint. Turning the "half empty" glass into a "half full" one is an obvious example of how a negative viewpoint can be transformed into a positive one. Reframing can work in the other direction, too. An action a client engaged in that he or she felt fine about until the clinician said, "How could you let yourself do that?" could rapidly turn her comfort into pain.

Most interventions, though, are intended to transform pain into comfort. The underlying assumption in doing reframing as an intervention strategy is that every experience (i.e., thought, feeling, behavior) has some positive value somewhere. By taking an experience that the client views as negative and commenting on how and why that same experience might actually be an asset to him or her in the proper context, the therapist can change the client's attitude about that experience, and the negativity can be discharged (Bandler & Grinder, 1979, 1982; Gilligan, 1987; Watzlawick, Weakland & Fisch, 1974).

Consider someone who believes that life is a clear-cut, black-or-white phenomenon. By thinking in such rigid extremes, the person thinks in terms of "must," "should," and what "the right way" is to do whatever. As a reframing, I might offer something like the following suggestions:

> Almost everyone has seen the inkblot tests some psychologists use...the client sees an inkblot...an ambiguous stimulus...and gives it meaning...from within himself...it's a projection...after all...the inkblot doesn't really mean anything...just what you think it means...and what is the most ambiguous stimulus any human being ever faces?...Life!...Life is an inkblot...lived out every day of your life...and some see life as an adventure...an opportunity...and some see it as a problem to endure until death...

To reframe "life as an inkblot" to counter the "life as black or white" redefines the meaning of life. Reframing means redefining.

SYMPTOM PRESCRIPTION

Symptom prescription as a therapeutic strategy involves the direct or indirect encouragement of the client's symptom(s). When the client is encouraged to do what he or she is already doing, but in some prescribed way that is slightly different through some shift (such as time or place of the symptomatic behavior), the symptom is experienced differently. When prescribed, the symptom is no longer a puzzling thing that "just happens," but rather it now arises in response to the clinician's direction. The spontaneous aspect of the symptom is now deliberate, and the problem pattern is interrupted. Consequently, it loses its original meaning and associations.

The applications of the symptom prescription paradigm are broad in scope. Encouraging a "resistant" person to "be resistant" redefines that resistance as cooperation. Encouraging a client to have a relapse redefines a relapse (unless the client resists and refuses to have one, which is better yet) as an acceptable and required part of the treatment process. Encouraging clients to do what they are already doing can give what seems like an uncontrolled symptom some concrete defining limits that make it a little easier for clients to deal with it effectively. The symptom that was out of the clients's control now comes under yours—and you can feel free to alter it a beneficial way (Haley, 1973; Seltzer, 1986; Weeks, 1991; Zeig, 1980a, 1980b).

THERAPEUTIC METAPHORS

Therapeutic metaphors are stories that can be created in such a way as to parallel the client's problems, and may be told in such a way as to deeply absorb the client. Often, the client may project meanings into the story that the clinician didn't even intend to communicate that can have greater impact than the intended meanings!

Learning to tell stories in a hypnotic manner (i.e., meaningfully, utilizing the client's responses, embedding suggestions, etc.) is a skill that is invaluable. The necessity of inducing a formal state of hypnosis diminishes as more and more hypnotic responses are obtained as the story is first introduced and then developed. The natural ability of the client to drift in and out of hypnosis as he or she listens to the clinician can be tapped and amplified by the clinician wanting to use a metaphorical approach. An implication of this approach is that change can, at times, be relatively effortless, a possibility that the clinician can allow for. After all, some changes do take place rather "spontaneously" (Barker, 1985; Brown, 1993; Gordon, 1980; Haley, 1973; Hammond, 1990; Lankton & Lankton, 1983, 1986, 1989; Mills & Crowley, 1986; Rosen, 1982; Spiegelman, 1990; Zeig, 1980c).

The following is an example of a therapeutic metaphor; one that might be appropriate to offer to someone who is responding rigidly to changing life circumstances he or she must be able to adapt to (e.g., job change or the like):

> ...and sometime in your life you've had the experience of going to the zoo...a wonderful place to learn about living life well...if you think about it...because the zoo contains such incredible diversity of life...and richness of life...all the unique creatures...each with different characteristics that serve them in some way...and you discover that some animals survive...by evolving to a huge size...and

some thrive by developing a small size...some succeed by feeding at night...and some by day...some are meek and frighten easily...others are aggressive and will charge others many times their size...some change colors to blend in...some burrow beneath the ground...while others fly...how wonderful to rise above it all...and the lesson from nature is a profound one...you can adapt to a climate...you can adapt to a region... you can adapt to particular place...and evolve the ability to thrive over time...and the lesson can also seem harsh...adapt or become extinct...but there is nothing hidden...about the value of successfully adapting...and enjoying all made possible by doing so...

CONCLUSION

In working with hypnosis, the clinician assumes an active role in facilitating experiences that can prove therapeutic for the client. There are literally thousands of therapeutic strategies available in the literature of hypnosis and psychotherapy. Those contained in this chapter are simply among the most commonly used.

REFERENCES

Araoz, D. (1985). *The new hypnosis*. New York: Brunner/Mazel.

Bandler, R. & Grinder, J. (1979). *Frogs into princes*. Moab, UT: Real People Press.

Bandler, R. & Grinder, J. (1982). *Reframing: Neuro-Linguistic Programming and the transformation of meaning*. Moab, UT: Real People Press.

Barker, P. (1985). *Using metaphors in psychotherapy*. New York: Brunner/Mazel.

Brown, P. (1993). Hypnosis and metaphor. In J. Rhue, S. Lynn & I. Kirsch (Eds.), *Handbook of clinical hypnosis* (pp. 291–308). Washington, DC: American Psychological Association.

Cheek, D. (1994). *Hypnosis: The application of ideomotor techniques*. Boston, MA: Allyn & Bacon.

Erickson, M. & Kubie, L. (1941). The successful treatment of a case of acute hysterical depression by a return under hypnosis to a critical phase of childhood. *Psychoanalytic Quarterly, 10*, 583–609.

Erickson, M. & Rossi, E. (1989). *The February man: Evolving consciousness and identity in hypnotherapy*. New York: Brunner/Mazel.

Feldman, S. (1985). Abreaction revisited: A strategic and interpersonal perspective. In J. Zeig (Ed.), *Ericksonian hypnotherapy:Vol 1, Structures* (pp. 338–358). New York: Brunner/Mazel.

Gilligan, S. (1987). *Therapeutic trances: The cooperation principle in Ericksonian hypnotherapy*. New York: Brunner/Mazel.

Gilligan, S. (1988). Symptom phenomena as trance phenomena. In J. Zeig & S. Lankton (Eds.), *Developing Ericksonian therapy: State of the art* (pp. 327–352).

New York: Brunner/Mazel.

Gordon, D. (1980). *Therapeutic metaphors.* Cupertino, CA: Meta Publications.

Haley, J. (1973). *Uncommon therapy.* New York: Norton.

Haley, J. (1984). *Ordeal therapy.* San Francisco: Jossey-Bass.

Hammond, D. (Ed.) (1990). *Handbook of hypnotic suggestions and metaphors.* New York: Norton.

Lankton, C. (1988). Task assignments: Logical and otherwise. In J. Zeig & S. Lankton (Eds.), *Developing Ericksonian therapy: State of the art* (pp. 257–279). New York: Brunner/Mazel.

Lankton, S. & Lankton, C. (1983). *The answer within: A clinical framework of Ericksonian hypnotherapy.* New York: Brunner/Mazel.

Lankton, S. & Lankton, C. (1986). *Enchantment and intervention in family therapy.* New York: Brunner/Mazel.

Lankton, S. & Lankton, C. (1989). *Tales of enchantment: Goal-oriented metaphors for adults and children in therapy.* New York: Brunner/Mazel.

Madanes, C. (1981). *Strategic family therapy.* San Francisco: Jossey-Bass.

Madanes, C. (1984). *Behind the one-way mirror: Advances in the practice of strategic therapy.* San Francisco: Jossey-Bass.

Mills, J. & Crowley, R. (1986). *Therapeutic metaphors for children and the child within.* New York: Brunner/Mazel.

Rosen, S. (Ed.) (1982). *My voice will go with you.* New York: Norton.

Seltzer, L. (1986). *Paradoxical strategies in psychotherapy.* New York: John Wiley & Sons.

Spiegel, D. (1993). Hypnosis in the treatment of post-traumatic stress disorders. In J. Rhue, S. Lynn & I. Kirsch (Eds.), *Handbook of clinical hypnosis* (pp. 493–508). Washington, DC: American Psychological Association.

Spiegel, H. & Spiegel, D. (1987). *Trance and treatment: Clinical uses of hypnosis.* Washington, DC: American Psychiatric Press.

Spiegelman, E. (1990). *Metaphor and meaning in psychotherapy.* New York: Guilford.

Watzlawick, P., Weakland, J. & Fisch, R. (1974). *Change.* New York: Norton.

Weeks, G. (Ed.) (1991). *Promoting change through paradoxical therapy* (Rev. ed.). New York: Brunner/Mazel.

Yapko, M. (1988). *When living hurts: Directives for treating depression.* New York: Brunner/Mazel.

Yapko, M. (1992). *Hypnosis and the treatment of depressions.* New York: Brunner/Mazel.

Zeig, J. (1980a). Symptom prescription and Ericksonian principles of hypnosis and psychotherapy. *American Journal of Clinical Hypnosis, 23*, 16–23.

Zeig, J. (1980b). Symptom prescription techniques: Clinical applications using elements of communication. *American Journal of Clinical Hypnosis, 23*, 23–32.

Zeig, J. (Ed.) (1980c). *A teaching seminar with Milton H. Erickson, M.D.* New York: Brunner/Mazel.

Zeig, J. (1988). An Ericksonian phenomenological approach to therapeutic hypnotic inductions and symptom utilization. In J. Zeig & S. Lankton (Eds.), *Developing Ericksonian therapy: State of the art* (pp. 353–375). New York: Brunner/Mazel.

20

HYPNOSIS IN THE TREATMENT OF COMMON DISORDERS

In clinical practice one encounters a wide range of presenting problems. Some are relatively rare, others are quite common. In this chapter is a brief and extremely superficial consideration of some of the most common clinical problems and some of the problems most frequently associated with hypnotic treatment. How hypnosis might be used directly and indirectly in their treatment is discussed.

ANXIETY DISORDERS (ANXIETY, STRESS, PHOBIAS, POST-TRAUMATIC STRESS DISORDER)

Hypnosis as a management tool can help build relaxation skills and a sense of self control. I believe teaching clients the skill of self-hypnosis (hypnotic inductions and utilizations they can perform on themselves whenever they'd like) is a necessary part of using hypnosis in clinical contexts. Simply knowing you have the ability to relax deeply and reorganize your thoughts, feelings, and behaviors can have a powerful effect in helping you manage your stress and anxiety. After all, the stress is often in the client's interpretation of events, not just in the events themselves. Hypnosis can facilitate alternate perspectives and thus alternate responses (Bandler, 1985; Brown & Fromm, 1987; Crawford & Barabasz, 1993; Habeck & Sheikh, 1984; Spiegel, 1993a; Yapko, 1989).

DEPRESSION

Depression is a very complex multidimensional problem that virtually all people experience from time to time in varying degrees. Addressing the depressed person's relationship problems, cognitive distortions, faulty attributions, and other depressogenic patterns with hypnotically based methods can be an effective approach.

Hypnosis may be used superficially to soothe anxiety, interrupt negative rumination, increase responsiveness, and establish positive expectancy. It may be used more intensively to facilitate flexibility in rigid, distorted patterns of thinking or interpreting events, reframe meanings attached to experiences rooted in faulty belief systems, and build positive frames of reference for responding to life from a more effective framework (Burrows, 1980; Havens & Walters, 1989; Havens, 1986; Miller, 1984; Torem, 1992; Yapko, 1988, 1989, 1992a, 1992b).

MULTIPLE PERSONALITY DISORDER (MPD)

Once considered an extremely rare disorder, MPD has been portrayed in some clinical literature as a far more common disorder than many clinicians realize. It is a highly controversial diagnosis, for despite its inclusion in the Diagnostic and Statistical Manual, 4th edition (DSM-IV), there are still many clinicians who openly question whether the dissociation evident in such cases might not be a product, at least in some cases, of the clinician's methods.

It is generally believed that MPD has its origin in severe childhood trauma (e.g., physical, sexual abuse) where dissociative reactions ("fragmentation") are employed as a coping mechanism. It has been shown that individuals suffering MPD are highly hypnotizable and fantasy prone (Frankel, 1990; Frischholz, 1985; Lynn, Rhue & Green, 1988).

Hypnosis is used with MPD to explore the range and quality of the client's dissociations, to reframe trauma, to "work through" traumatic memories, to facilitate integration, and to address related symptoms (Bliss, 1986; Braun, 1986; Horevitz, 1993; Kluft, 1985; Kluft & Fine, 1993; Putnam, 1989; Ross, 1989).

PAIN, DISEASE, HEALING

From the earlier section on analgesia and anesthesia, you already have some familiarity with the fact that hypnosis can be used to reduce or eliminate pain and suffering. The most common misconception people hold is that if you can alter the person's perception of pain with hypnosis, then the pain wasn't "real," meaning it must have been "psychological" (i.e., psychogenic). In fact, hypnosis can be used as a sole or principal anesthetic even in major surgeries, where the tissue damage is clearly evident and physically based. How performing an induction and utilizing any or all of the dozens of pain management strategies can create a state that allows one to tolerate surgery with no anesthetic is anybody's guess (this is a current focus of much research), but it is truly a real, even if amazing, phenomenon.

Whether the pain is acute or chronic, from a known organic disease or injury or from an unknown, perhaps psychogenic, source is of little consequence to the effective use of hypnosis to reduce pain and suffering (Brown & Fromm, 1987; Chaves, 1993; Erickson, 1959, 1966; Hammond, 1990; Hilgard & Hilgard, 1994; Spanos & Chaves, 1989).

Hypnosis has been applied successfully in the treatment of a wide variety of medical problems, including burns, cancer, asthma, allergies, tinnitus, hypertension, warts, and almost any other medical problem you can think of. Hypnosis may enhance the quality and rate of recovery, it may help one maintain a sense of control over one's condition (curtailing depression and anxiety), or it may simply be a placebo that is found to be helpful.

Does hypnosis "cure" cancer, AIDS, or any other disease? What about hypnosis and healing? This is a highly controversial area in the world of clinical hypnosis. There are many anecdotal reports of cancer remission and apparent cures following hypnotic treatment. There is a growing body of objective evidence that the use of hypnosis *can* enhance the body's natural defense system, the immune system (Spiegel, 1993b). The message, "You can heal yourself with the right attitude" is a popular one for obvious reasons, and so it is a powerful lure for the sick and dying. The most ethical practitioners are clear that they cannot say, "I will cure your cancer" (or whatever), but they are equally clear that there is potentially much to be gained from trying. Walking the tightrope between fostering what may be a false belief in a cure and keeping the positive attitude that a cure may be possible is a distinct challenge for the practitioner of methods of mind-body healing (Benjamin & Trubo, 1987; Chopra, 1991; Jevne & Levitan, 1989; Pearsall, 1987; Rossi, 1993; Rossi & Cheek, 1988; Siegel, 1986; Simonton, Henson & Hampton, 1992).

RELATIONSHIP PROBLEMS (COUPLES, FAMILIES)

Often, the partners in a relationship have inadequate communication skills, ill-defined or inappropriate expectations, poor self-esteem, fears of intimacy or commitment, and other such barriers to an effective relationship.

Hypnotic strategies may be employed to clarify expectations, increase the level of motivation to resolve differences within the relationship, enhance communication skills, and resolve unconscious conflicts about intimacy and commitment. Metaphorical approaches, symptom prescription, and reframing are effective patterns to use in relationship counseling. Changing personal history is a good strategy to use in working individually with someone who experiences relationship problems, building in the resources necessary to effectively relate to another person. Helping the person to clarify what he or she really wants and values is a good starting point for any clinical problem, but is especially necessary in the context of relationship counseling (Haley, 1973; Kershaw, 1992; Lankton & Lankton, 1986; Protinsky, 1988; Ritterman, 1983, 1985).

SELF-ESTEEM PROBLEMS

When you work with self-esteem problems hypnotically, your client can be encouraged to take control of situations by planning and executing a course of action very efficiently. Clients often berate themselves with a steady stream of self-criticisms. Good self-esteem does *not* mean there is no "inner critic," it just means the person doesn't accept what it says as true or get absorbed in it as though it was the sum total of their being. Good self-esteem allows you to downplay or even ignore the inner critic. Good self-esteem also means not confusing who you are with what you do. The first reframing in treating self-esteem is to say, "It isn't you— it's the way you go about trying to do X." When people learn successful strategies for doing X, their self-esteem can improve.

You can engage the client's attention with metaphor intensely as he or she learns about another person's experiences: how the person in the metaphor experienced the same or structurally similar problems, how he or she handled it, and what the consequences were. Through a therapeutic metaphor, the client can acquire learnings that have a greater impact than does simply stating the story's point. The metaphor can match to whatever degree the clinician desires the client's frame of reference, feelings, level of experience, and unconscious dynamics. Once an identification is built through such matching, the therapeutic metaphor can go on to suggest solutions, encourage actions, and embed suggestions (Alman & Lambrou, 1992; Hammond, 1990; Lankton & Lankton, 1983; McNeal & Frederick, 1993).

SEXUAL DYSFUNCTIONS

People with sexual problems are often in a dissociated state relative to their sexual functioning. There is a part of them attempting to engage in sexual activity, and another part that is observing and criticizing performance. The result is diffuse concentration that dissipates the focused state necessary to function well sexually. Hypnosis may be employed to facilitate the process of reintegration so that *all* of the person may be in the "here-and-now," experiencing and enjoying the sexual activity. One intervention involves altering sensory awareness by heightening kinesthetic sensitivity hypnotically. This is essentially an amplified sensate-focus technique that more traditional sex therapists employ in the treatment of sexual dysfunction.

Anxiety about sexual performance is a primary target for hypnotic intervention in cases of sexual dysfunction. Anxiety causes poor performance, which causes more anxiety, which then escalates the probability of poor performance and so on in a vicious circle. Using the comfort of hypnosis to allow the client to "let go" is a good model for "letting go" during sexual activity—fundamental to sexual enjoyment. Teaching self-hypnosis to help clients master the anxiety allows the relaxation to generalize to the context where they would like to have it.

Reframing sex as a natural, healthy function is one more use for hypnotic patterns in sexual therapy. Giving the paradoxical directive to "avoid sex at all costs this week" can facilitate the "I'll show you by doing it" attitude in the client. Changing personal history to reteach a positive attitude toward sex is also a viable treatment strategy. Age progressing the client to see himself or herself sexually active and satisfied is yet another potential application of hypnosis. Hypnosis and sex therapy are two highly compatible and easily integrated approaches to the treatment of sexual dysfunctions (Araoz, 1982, 1984; Crasilneck, 1982, 1990; Erickson, 1973; Hammond, 1990; Zeig, 1980).

SUBSTANCE ABUSE (SMOKING, WEIGHT, DRUGS)

Hypnosis can be used to recultivate body awareness and build self-esteem and a sense of independence such that *whatever* situations you encounter, they can be dealt with without self-abuse. The clinician can make the experience of engaging in substance abuse terribly inconvenient, resolve any underlying depression so common yet so infrequently diagnosed among substance abusers (frequently the substance abuse is self-medication for the anxiety associated with depression), and even hypnotically recreate the good feelings of the substance without actually ingesting it.

Resolving substance abuse problems can be a process of reintegrating the dissociated elements and reframing both the meaning of the self-destructive behavior and the implications of the client's beliefs system (Alman &Lambrou, 1992; Hammond, 1990; Levitt, 1993; Lynn, Neufeld,

Rhue & Matorin, 1993; Orman, 1991; Page & Handley, 1993; Spiegel & Spiegel, 1987; Zeig, 1985).

CONCLUSION

Learning how, when, and where to apply the many different potential therapeutic experiences that are available through hypnosis requires years of practice and study. This chapter aimed to expose the student of clinical hypnosis to a few of the many ways hypnosis may be creatively and meaningfully applied. The deeper your understanding of the numerous components that are a part of each and every symptom, the greater the respect you can have for the overall integrity of the finely balanced system called "the client."

REFERENCES

Alexander, L. (1974). Treatment of impotency and anorgasmia by psychotherapy aided by hypnosis. *American Journal of Clinical Hypnosis, 17*, 33–43.

Alman, D. & Lambrou, P. (1992). *Self-hypnosis: The complete manual for health and self-change.* New York: Brunner/Mazel.

Araoz, D. (1982). *Hypnosis and sex therapy.* New York: Brunner/Mazel.

Araoz, D. (1984). Hypnosis in the treatment of sexual dysfunctions. In W. Wester & A. Smith (Eds.), *Clinical Hypnosis: A multidisciplinary approach* (pp. 405–420). Philadelphia: Lippincott.

Araoz, D. (1988). Human sexuality, hypnosis, and therapy. In J. Zeig & S. Lankton (Eds.), *Developing Ericksonian therapy: State of the art* (pp. 438–445). New York: Brunner/Mazel.

Bandler, R. (1985). *Using your brain—for a change.* C. Andreas & S. Andreas (Eds.). Moab, UT: Real People Press.

Benjamin, H. & Trubo, R. (1987). *From victim to victor: The wellness community guide to fighting for recovery for cancer patients and their families.* Los Angeles: Tarcher.

Bliss, E. (1986). *Multiple personality, allied disorders, and hypnosis.* New York: Oxford University Press.

Braun, B. (1986). *Treatment of multiple personality disorder.* Washington, DC: American Psychiatric Press.

Brown, D. & Fromm, E. (1987). *Hypnosis and behavioral medicine.* Hillsdale, NJ: Erlbaum.

Burrows, G. (1980). Affective disorders and hypnosis. In G. Burrows & L. Dennerstein (Eds.), *Handbook of hypnosis and psychosomatic medicine* (pp. 149–170). Amsterdam: Elsevier/North-Holland Biomedical Press.

Chaves, J. (1993). Hypnosis in pain management. In J. Rhue, S. Lynn & I. Kirsch (Eds.), *Handbook of clinical hypnosis* (pp. 511–532). Washington, DC: American Psychological Association.

Chopra, D. (1991). *Perfect health: The complete mind/body guide.* New York: Random House.

Crasilneck, H. (1982). A follow-up study in the use of hypnotherapy in the treatment of psychogenic impotency. *American Journal of Clinical Hypnosis, 25,* 52–61.

Crasilneck, H. (1990). Hypnotic techniques for smoking control and psychogenic impotence. *American Journal of Clinical Hypnosis, 32,* 147–153.

Crawford, H. & Barabasz, A. (1993). Phobias and intense fears: Facilitating their treatment with hypnosis. In J. Rhue, S. Lynn & I. Kirsch (Eds.), *Handbook of clinical hypnosis* (pp. 311–337). Washington, DC:American Psychological Association.

Erickson, M. (1959). Hypnosis in painful terminal illness. *American Journal of Clinical Hypnosis, 1,* 117–121.

Erickson, M. (1966). The interspersal hypnotic technique for symptom correction and pain control. *American Journal of Clinical Hypnosis, 8,* 198–209.

Erickson, M. (1973). Psychotherapy achieved by a reversal of the neurotic processes in a case of ejaculation praecox. *American Journal of Clinical Hypnosis, 15,* 219–221.

Frankel, F. (1990). Hypnotizability and dissociation. *American Journal of Psychiatry, 147,* 823–829.

Frischholz, E. (1985). The relationship among dissociation, hypnosis, and child abuse in the development of multiple personality disorder. In R. Kluft (Ed.), *Childhood antecedents of multiple personality disorder* (pp. 100–126). Washington, DC: American Psychiatric Press.

Habeck, B. & Sheikh, A. (1984). Imagery and the treatment of phobic disorders. In A. Sheikh (Ed.), *Imagination and healing* (pp. 171–196). Farmingdale, NY: Baywood.

Haley, J. (1973). *Uncommon therapy.* New York: Norton.

Hammond, D. (Ed.) (1990). *Handbook of hypnotic suggestions and metaphors.* New York: Norton.

Havens, R. (1986). Posthypnotic predetermination of therapeutic progress. *American Journal of Clinical Hypnosis, 28,* 258–262.

Havens, R. & Walters, C. (1989). *Hypnotherapy scripts: A neo-Ericksonian approach to persuasive healing.* New York: Brunner/Mazel.

Hilgard, E. & Hilgard, J. (1994). *Hypnosis in the relief of pain.* New York: Brunner/Mazel.

Horevitz, R. (1993). Hypnosis in the treatment of multiple personality disorder. In J. Rhue, S. Lynn & I. Kirsch (Eds.), *Handbook of clinical hypnosis* (pp. 395–424). Washington, DC: American Psychological Association.

Jevne, R. & Levitan, A. (1989). *No time for nonsense: Self-help for the seriously ill.* San Diego, CA: Lura Media.

Kershaw, C. (1992). *The couple's hypnotic dance.* New York: Brunner/Mazel.

Kluft, R. (Ed.) (1985). *Childhood antecedents of multiple personality.* Washington, DC: American Psychiatric Press.

Kluft, R. & Fine, C. (Eds.) (1993). *Clinical perspectives on multiple personality disorder.* Washington, DC: American Psychiatric Press.

Lankton, S. & Lankton, C. (1983). *The answer within: A clinical framework of Ericksonian hypnotherapy.* New York: Brunner/Mazel.

Lankton, S. & Lankton, C. (1986). *Enchantment and intervention in family therapy.* New York: Brunner/Mazel.

Levitt, E. (1993). Hypnosis in the treatment of obesity. In J. Rhue, S. Lynn & I. Kirsch (Eds.), *Handbook of clinical hypnosis* (pp. 533–553). Washington, DC: American Psychological Association.

Lynn, S., Neufeld, V., Rhue, J. & Matorin, A. (1993). Hypnosis and smoking cessation: A cognitive-behavioral treatment. In J. Rhue, S. Lynn & I. Kirsch (Eds.), *Handbook of clinical hypnosis* (pp. 555–585). Washington, DC: American Psychological Association.

Lynn, S., Rhue, J. & Green, J. (1988). Multiple personality and fantasy proneness: Is there an association or dissociation? *British Journal of Experimental and Clinical Hypnosis, 5,* 138–142.

McNeal,S. & Frederick, C. (1993). Inner strength and other techniques for ego strengthening. *American Journal of Clinical Hypnosis, 35,* 170–178.

Miller, H. (1984). Depression—A specific cognitive pattern. In W. Wester & A. Smith (Eds.), *Clinical hypnosis: A multidisciplinary approach* (pp. 421–457). Philadelphia: Lippincott.

Orman, D. (1991). Reframing of an addiction via hypnotherapy: A case presentation. *American Journal of Clinical Hypnosis, 33,* 263–271.

Page, R. & Handley, G. (1993). The use of hypnosis in cocaine addiction. *American Journal of Clinical Hypnosis, 36,* 120–123.

Pearsall, P. (1987). *Superimmunology: Master your emotions and improve your health.* New York: McGraw-Hill.

Protinsky, H. (1988). Hypnotic strategies in strategic marital therapy. *Journal of Strategic and Systemic Therapies, 7,* 29–34.

Putnam, F. (1989). *Diagnosis and treatment of multiple personality disorder.* New York: Guilford.

Ritterman, M. (1983). *Using hypnosis in family therapy.* San Francisco: Jossey-Bass.

Ritterman, M. (1985). Family context symptom induction and therapeutic counterinduction: Breaking the spell of a dysfunctional rapport. In J. Zeig (Ed.), *Ericksonian psychotherapy: Vol. 2, Clinical applications.* New York: Brunner/Mazel.

Ross, C. (1989). *Multiple personality disorder: Diagnosis, clinical features and treatment.* New York: John Wiley & Sons.

Rossi, E. (1993). *The psychobiology of mind-body healing* (Rev. ed.). New York: Norton.

Rossi, E. & Cheek, D. (1988). *Mind-body therapy: Methods of ideodynamic healing in hypnosis.* New York: Norton.

Siegel, B. (1986). *Love, medicine and miracles.* New York: Harper & Row.

Simonton, O., Henson, R. & Hampton, F. (1992). *The healing journey.* New York: Bantam.

Spanos, N. & Chaves, J. (1989). Hypnotic analgesia, surgery and reports of nonvolitional pain. *British Journal of Experimental and Clinical Hypnosis, 6,* 131–139.

Spiegel, D. (1993a). Hypnosis in the treatment of post-traumatic stress disorders. In J. Rhue, S. Lynn & I. Kirsch (Eds.), *Handbook of clinical hypnosis* (pp. 493–508). Washington, DC: American Psychological Association.

Spiegel, D. (1993b). *Living beyond limits.* New York: Times Books.

Spiegel, H. & Spiegel, D. (1987). *Trance and treatment: Clinical uses of hypnosis.* Washington, DC: American Psychiatric Press.

Torem, M. (1992). "Back from the future": A powerful age-progression technique. *American Journal of Clinical Hypnosis, 35,* 81–88.

Yapko, M. (1988). *When living hurts: Directives for treating depression.* New York: Brunner/Mazel.

Yapko, M. (Ed.) (1989). *Brief therapy approaches to treating anxiety and depression.* New York: Brunner/Mazel.

Yapko, M. (1992a). *Free yourself from depression.* Emmaus, PA: Rodale Press.

Yapko, M. (1992b). *Hypnosis and the treatment of depressions.* New York: Brunner/Mazel.

Zeig, J. (Ed.) (1980). *A teaching seminar with Milton H. Erickson, M.D.* New York: Brunner/Mazel.

Zeig, J. (1985). Ericksonian approaches to promote abstinence from cigarette smoking. In J. Zeig (Ed.), *Ericksonian psychotherapy, Vol. 1, Structures* (pp. 255–269). New York: Brunner/Mazel.

21

A SAMPLE TRANCE-SCRIPT: BUILDING BOUNDARIES

The hypnotic process in this chapter relates to the issues associated with establishing and maintaining a clear sense of personal boundaries. How well one defines one's boundaries comprises a key component of personal experience. When I talk about boundaries, I refer to one's ability to separate one's own experience from that of others, as well as the ability to break global experiences into their component parts. Clarity about what separates one person from another or one experience from another allows one to selectively focus on and amplify a particular dimension of experience, or, likewise, to focus away from, and therefore minimize one's awareness for a different dimension of experience.

One common pattern of thinking that underlies many problems is a tendency towards what is called "global thinking." The global thinker, metaphorically speaking, sees the forest, but not the trees. The global thinker may see the big picture, but not the smaller component elements that come together to form the big picture. Consequently, the global thinker tends to have a difficult time separating his or her experience into various components in order to be able to focus on them sequentially and in some reasonable order of priority. For example, this is why some individuals complain about feeling overwhelmed. They are, typically, globally aware of *all* the problems they face in life seemingly all at once, which would be overwhelming for *anyone*. Thus, it becomes a specific goal in treatment to teach the person not only to identify all the problems, but to achieve some sense of priority and establish a sensible sequence in which the problems are going to be addressed, followed by specific strategies for how they will be addressed.

This tape transcript is featured in the *Using Hypnosis in the Treatment of Depression* audiotape set by Michael D. Yapko (Brunner/Mazel, 1992).

A particular cognitive skill known as "compartmentalization" involves the ability to separate elements of experience effectively. This skill can serve a person in many ways. It means, for example, that in your relationship with yourself, you are able to separate your thoughts from your feelings. Or, that you are able to separate your impulses from your actions, or that you are able to separate your personal life from your professional life. By establishing definite boundaries that clearly define each part of who you are, you are better able to choose which part of yourself you are going to respond to in a particular situation. If you think about the kinds of problems that you experience or see other people experience, so often it's because the person tends to get wrapped up in an element of experience that works against him or her. Consider, as an example, the person who is going to get on an airplane to travel somewhere and then starts generating terrible and detailed images of plane crashes in his or her mind. That's *not* the most useful image to focus on at that particular moment. The fact that a person has the images isn't so much the problem. Most people will consider the negative possibilities to some extent (if only because they are required to as the flight attendant reviews emergency procedures prior to departure), but they differ in how much they'll focus on them and amplify them.

Consider another example: What happens when you find yourself attracted to someone you know is wrong for you, or perhaps desiring an expensive item you can't afford? What happens when your heart is clearly telling you "yes," but intellectually, and at a more logical level, you are aware that the situation is too hazardous and that you really should let the opportunity pass? In other words, what happens when your heart says "yes" and your head says "no"? Compartmentalization and clear boundaries would allow you to skillfully separate your feelings from your thoughts and actions and *do what will prove to be the best thing in the long run*—something that you will also feel better for having done. Clearly, compartmentalization is related to a future orientation, namely thinking ahead. It underlies the skill that is generally known as "impulse control."

In the same way that boundaries are very important in defining your relationship with yourself internally, boundaries are equally important in regulating your relationships with others. It may seem obvious that someone else's experience isn't your experience, yet what happens so commonly is that individuals react to other people as if they're the same as or are extensions of themselves. You have to be able to clearly separate what is you from what is someone else. For example, if I tell you that "I think you are too aggressive as a person," does that mean that you really are too aggressive? Why would I say that about you? Certainly, you would have to consider, at least for a moment, my feedback that perhaps you *are* too aggressive. You would stop and review our interactions and you would then consider whether my observation is valid. But you also have to go a step further in your thinking and clarify the boundaries between you and me. You have to be able to ask yourself questions like, "Why would Michael say I'm too aggressive? Is there something about Michael's experience—independent of me—that would lead him to say that?" Simply by asking that second question, you start to establish the distinctions between you and your experience and me and my experience. On one hand, you'd have to consider that you are too aggressive, but on the other hand, you'd have to consider that perhaps I'm a wimp who gets intimidated too easily, and that's why I find you too aggressive.

Now, consider the difference in these two interpretations. In the first case, you define yourself as too aggressive, accepting my feedback to you uncritically. In the second case, you realize my comment is as much a statement about me and my feelings as it is about you, even though I said it is about you. The task is to look for evidence to validate one interpretation over another, and not just accept uncritically what I've said about you.

Boundaries separate and define relationships. That means that the roles we are in at any given moment help define more clearly what is and what is not possible between us. I can serve as someone's clinical psychologist, but if I'm going to be this person's psychologist, should I also be his or her personal friend? No! A line clearly separates those two very different relationships. If I am someone's psychologist, I am not also that person's friend because this is a professional relationship requiring my clarity in order that I may be able to give the person objective feedback without the emotional considerations and the kind of easy familiarity that go along with personal friendship. Consider being a parent. Do you want to be your young child's parent? Or, do you want to be your young child's friend? There is a line that separates those roles, and you cannot effectively do both.

The goal of the following noninteractional hypnotic process is to help one draw clear lines and then protect those lines, meaning you set limits and protect those limits. Certainly, you must know that other people will constantly attempt to push you to collapse your boundaries. People will always want your time, your money, your body, your expertise, your support, your *something*.... And so, you'll likely encounter the boss who wants a personal relationship, or the teacher who wants to be your parent, or the parent who wants to be your friend. The fact that other people's boundaries are so weak that they will attempt to collapse the boundaries between you and them is hardly noteworthy, because that's just what people do. People use each other for personal gain. When it's a win-win situation, it can be pretty healthy. But, when it's someone using you for his or her personal gain to your detriment, it's no longer a healthy situation. So, it's important as an additional goal in this process that you learn to recognize other people's manipulative efforts and manipulative tactics. These are the methods others use to get you to collapse your boundaries, the ways in which they attempt to control you through tactics like guilt, flattery, seduction, anger and intimidation, or withdrawal from you by turning a cold shoulder. There are obviously many tactics for getting an individual to comply with one's wishes and thereby give up any sense of personal boundaries that he or she might have. You are the only person who can protect yourself from others' manipulations. But, you can only do that well if you have a very clear sense of your own boundaries.

The hypnotic process presented here is meant to help you get a sense of who you really are and come to know what all the different parts of you are all about and to use them effectively in each and every situation that you face. Each part of you is valuable, and so sometimes you can follow your heart, and other times you'll want to follow your head. Sometimes, you'll be able to follow your impulses, and other times you'll have to be able to think your way past your impulses. There are no formulas for living life well and feeling good; instead, you can make an appraisal of what's going to work best for you in any given situation based on the outcome you are striving for.

> Now, let's begin...you can arrange yourself in a position that is comfortable and start to orient yourself now...to what is by now probably a familiar experience...of allowing yourself to get comfortably relaxed...letting yourself get absorbed in different ideas...and different ways of experiencing yourself...gradually notice...how it starts to become very clear to you...what is inside...that defines you as you...and what is outside...that goes on in the world out there...that you are always a part of...and yet paradoxically are always separate from...And so, now at the outset of this experience...as you let your eyes close...and you let your attention drift inwardly...you can be aware there are many different elements of experience...that you can focus your attention on...one part of who you are...is represented by the different thoughts that pass through your awareness...Whatever things that you think about...and whatever occurs to you...in reaction to the things that I describe...and also in response to your own thoughts...as one thought triggers another, which triggers another...as your

148 Essentials of Hypnosis

awareness skips from thought to thought...and place to place...All of that is mental experience...conscious experience...which is one very important part of who you are...There is also another part of you worth recognizing...namely the physical aspect of your experience...the feel of your body...as you rest so comfortably in the chair...Which part of your body...seems to relax first?...And at just what moment do you begin to notice...that your breathing is slowing down?...that your pulse rate is slowing down?...Which part of your body begins to feel the most distant?...And which part the closest?...There are so many different aspects of physical experience...And another valuable part of you...is the part that has feelings...about what I'm going to be talking about...curious about what you're going to be able to learn...and use...much to your own satisfaction...Your feelings of comfort...and being able to settle in...and enjoy...having some quiet times like now...without really having to think...without having to analyze...A time to just simply "be" for a while...Feelings of pleasure...feelings of pride in what you know...feelings of confidence you can learn...feelings of relaxation from not having to say anything...not having to do anything...And just how many parts of you are there?...There are optimistic parts...and pessimistic parts...parts that like to work...and parts that like to play...parts that like to think ahead...parts that like to think about what has been...parts that like to be with others...and parts that like to be alone...thinking parts...feelings parts...and so many that I could name hundreds of parts...and what you're coming to know now...is that each part of your experience...has wonderful potential...to be valuable...some time...some place...To know that you can move into...and get very absorbed in one part of experience...is a very valuable learning...It's as if the spotlight of your awareness...lights up a particular part of yourself...in a situation...and allows you to handle that situation skillfully...And you're also learning...how readily a mismatch between a part and a situation...can generate problems...You know, for example, that if you're going to go to a party...that it's certainly important to be able to reach inside yourself and bring out the social part of yourself...that part of you that likes people and takes enjoyment in being with people...That likes to laugh and joke...and hear other people's perspectives...and share in other people's experiences...Those are all the things that can make a party a lot of fun...but what would happen if someone were to go to a party...and get so very absorbed in an internal experience...like a bad mood...effectively separating...himself or herself from others?...And now you're learning...that there are times to get absorbed internally...introspectively...and there are times to get absorbed externally...To be absorbed internally at a party...isn't a very good match...and then the feelings will be hurtful...and negative...in evaluating oneself...on the way home...from the party...self-critically wondering...why you couldn't get into...the party frame of mind...There are walls in each person...walls that you can build up...and walls that you can tear down...on a moment's notice...Walls that separate...different parts of your experience from each other...as if each is in its own compartment...And you can easily imagine walking down a long hallway...with many doors on either side...so that if you open one particular door you can get into your thoughts...or if you open a different door you can get into your feelings...or if you open still another door you can get into your vulnerabilities...or if you open a different door you can get into your strengths...What an extraordinary sense of control...and personal power...when you know and appreciate all the different parts of yourself...and you know how to move...into and out of each...And isn't it valuable to be able to learn from others' experiences?...I remember working with one individual not long ago...who described how he lives with the woman he loves very much...But he notices how often in the mornings...before they're about to go off to work...and go their own separate ways for the day...how they'll get into small arguments...simple conflicts about who will stop to pick up milk on the way home...or who will stop and pick up a newspaper on the way home...And, they'll say things to each other that aren't particularly pleasant or polite or loving...He'll be devastated...and he'll get so upset that they argued that he can't even go to work...He's so confused about how they could have an argument...and that his girlfriend still goes off to work...How important it is that he learn...how to separate his personal life...from his work life...his personal feelings...from his ability to function...on the job...And even within himself...He needs to know how to separate his frustration and anger...from the things that he says to his girlfriend...in order to deal with the differences between them...however big or small they may be...in ways that are respectful...Internal feelings of rage can be separate from...saying things that are mean or destructive...There's a wall that separates your feelings from your actions...rage from violence...feelings of desire or attraction from behaving irresponsibly...And you're learning now...that you can separate different parts of your experience...That you can even separate your usual experience of yourself from your experience of yourself when you're doing hypnosis...And you can separate all the things that you have to do later today...from this experience you're having right now...of relaxing...and listening...and learning...Now, you know...that every country...every state...has its borders...There's a line...that separates...the United States from Canada...and the United States from Mexico...There's a line that separates...the state that you live in...from a neighboring state...and the city that you live in...from a neighboring city...The United States...even has...a border patrol...which has the task of maintaining the integrity of our borders...to keep in what needs to be kept in...and keep out what needs to be kept out...And it is our nation's job...to be able to protect our borders...in order to be able to define us...as us...Everywhere you go...each country has its borders...and its own way of defining itself...its culture...its language...its customs...Now, you know as well as I...how frequently...one group of people will invade another group...and cross the boundaries...and attempt to impose its will and its way of life...It's really no different at the individual level...how clearly you can begin to see...people seeking from you...the things that they want...And now it's you...and your boundaries...and your ability to protect those boundaries...that keep you from getting swept up in someone else's plans...Being able to easily resist...their tactics of guilt...or intimidation...or whatever...in order to be able to protect yourself...skillfully...carefully...powerfully...And so you're learning...faster than you even consciously realize...that every part of you is valuable...somewhere...some time...Whether it's an angry part...or a playful part...whether it's a loving part...or a critical part...It serves a valuable purpose...when you use it well...And what you're now learning...is that you can have the ability...to deliberately tap into a particular part of yourself...that's always your choice...So, that when you've done something that didn't go so well...you can find the compassionate part of yourself...and be absorbed in it...And when you're experiencing tension...you can find the part of you that knows how to relax...and get absorbed in it...And, when you find yourself being self-critical...you can find the part of you that knows how to be patient...and accepting...and you can revel in it...Your experience is yours and no one else's...And when you realize that...you come to understand that no matter how much someone loves you...that if you were to break your leg...you would have to wear the cast...no one can wear it for you...There is *always*...a boundary that separates you from others...And how very fortunate it is that life is that way...so that you can be you...so that you can develop all the different parts of yourself to their fullest...To know when to use them and how to use all those parts...in ways that you can feel wonderful about...And so, enjoy...the feelings of comfort...and take some time to process your experience...integrating new learnings...reinforcing familiar learnings...and using your experience skillfully...and then when you're ready, you can bring this experience to a comfortable close...reorienting gradually when you feel ready to...and then reorienting fully and opening your eyes when it seems like a good time to...

22

MEMORY, SUGGESTIBILITY, AND THE REPRESSED MEMORY CONTROVERSY

Consider a woman seeking psychotherapy who reports terrifying nightmares, an eating disorder, and difficulties in her interpersonal relationships, especially with men. She claims she has no idea what causes her symptoms, but her psychotherapist suggests to her directly that her symptoms indicate that she "must have been sexually abused and repressed the memories." She has no memories, or even hints of memories, for any such events.

Through hypnosis and hypnotically based techniques (visualization, guided imagery) of age regression, she soon recovers some memories of sexual abuse occurring at a very early age. Did these episodes of abuse actually happen? Might they have been manufactured unintentionally in order to accommodate the expectations and suggestions of the psychotherapist? Is it possible to lead someone to believe he or she was sexually abused when no such abuse ever actually occurred?

These difficult questions lie at the heart of one of the most heated controversies in the psychotherapy field today. On one side of the issue, we have those clinicians and researchers who believe that sexual abuse traumas that have been repressed can and should be readily identified from a known symptom check list (Blume, 1990; Fredrickson, 1992). They further believe that treatment should involve first lifting the veil of repression with a variety of memory recovery techniques, then working with the newly discovered traumatic material in order to help the client reach new symptom-free resolutions. They are also concerned that perpetrators of sexual abuse will be given a new basis for evading responsibility for their actions by dismissing allegations of abuse as the product of false memories. And, finally, they believe that memories recovered in psychotherapy are essentially true, and need to be acknowledged as such before treatment can succeed.

On the other side of the issue, we have those clinicians and researchers who are skeptical of anyone's professed ability to readily diagnose someone repressing memories of trauma on the basis of some symptom cluster that could be just as readily explained by other means (Ganaway, 1991; Loftus, 1993). After all, repression cannot be studied directly, it can only be inferred. (You cannot ask someone, "Are you repressing memories of abuse?" If he or she knows all about it, then it isn't repressed.) These clinicians and researchers further believe that by reaching a conclusion that the client has been abused and is repressing memories to that effect, psychotherapists can either intentionally or unintentionally influence the person to reach that same conclusion when it may not be true. They are concerned that innocent people will be falsely accused and their lives all but destroyed as a result. They recognize that people can be influenced, especially in some particularly vulnerable situations like psychotherapy, to believe damaging things that may have no basis in fact.

There has been increasing effort made to determine how responsive to suggestion memory might be. Studies by Laurence and Perry (1983); Orne (1979); Sheehan, Statham and Jamieson (1991); Lynn, Milano and Weekes (1992); and Loftus (1993) have all lent support to the recognition that *memory is reconstructive, not reproductive*. Thus, the accuracy of memory can be influenced by many factors, including suggestion and misinformation (Bower, 1981; Labelle, Laurence, Nadon & Perry, 1990; Loftus, 1980; Lynn, Weekes & Milano, 1989; Sheehan & Grigg, 1985).

As another such factor, repression is an especially complicating variable because its influence on the accuracy of memory is not yet fully understood (Loftus & Yapko, 1995). Specifically, it is not yet known how or even whether repression diminishes or enhances the accuracy of long-buried memories, and to what degree suggestive (hypnotic) procedures employed by psychotherapists to recover repressed memories might contaminate the memories derived from them (Dywan & Bowers, 1983; Kihlstrom & Evans, 1979; Laurence, Nadon, Nogrady & Perry, 1986; Loftus & Hoffman, 1989; Watkins, 1989).

When psychotherapists first suspect and then look intently for a history of abuse which has presumably been repressed in a particular client, their beliefs about memory and their awareness (or lack thereof) of themselves as suggestive influences are directly involved in the "search and rescue" mission. Believing, for example, that one can accurately store and later remember memories of conversations and experiences from the very first moments of life leads to different psychotherapy techniques than if one has no such belief (Yapko, 1990).

Unfortunately, many psychotherapists believe in past lives, the retrievability and accuracy of infantile memories, and the infallibility of hypnosis as a tool for recovering accurate memories (Yapko, 1994a). Many continue to maintain the rigid but unfounded belief that accurate memories of all experiences must be in there somewhere in one form or another, and that all one needs is the right "key" to "unlock" them. False memories that are detailed and dramatic may be accepted as true simply because of the psychotherapist's preexisting beliefs (Scheflin & Shapiro, 1989).

Without objective corroborating evidence like a photograph or video-tape, how can you distinguish a real memory from a confabulation? This question goes right to the heart of the matter, and the answer is quite discouraging: No objectively reliable method for doing so currently exists. This conclusion represents the unanimous response of many experts on both sides of the issue (Yapko, 1994a, 1994b).

The mental health profession does not yet know very much about the repression of traumatic memories. In fact, some question repression's very existence (Holmes, 1990). Does repression exist? The evidence strongly suggests that it does. But, clinicians do not yet know how common repression of childhood sexual abuse really is. We do not yet know the authenticity of memories that have been buried 20 or 30 years that suddenly and dramatically surface in response to a lecture, a self-help book, or a psychotherapy session. We do not know whether repressed memories always exist when symptoms are present, ever waiting to be uncovered as the source of that client's problems, or whether the same kind of symptoms can exist independently of negative experiences that might have been repressed. We do not know from what age repression is even possible. We do not know if trauma makes a repressed memory less or more accurate in a given individual. We do not know which techniques for recovering repressed memories will alter them in significant ways merely by their use. We do not know why some people repress a particular type of trauma and other do not. We do not know why some people never have traumatic memories, which are objectively known to exist in their backgrounds, surface in their aware-ness while others have memories that eventually do return. These many unknowns all represent areas badly in need of further research.

CLINICAL IMPLICATIONS

Dealing with these issues clinically is tricky. The remainder of this chapter provides some tips for handling these delicate matters. This section is reprinted with permission from a piece I wrote for a special issue of *The Family Therapy Networker* (Yapko, 1993a).

How are therapists to navigate the murky terrain between the obvious untruths and the undeniable reality that comprise so much of the practice of therapy? Suppose a client comes in and says, "I was hypnotized (or "did imagery work" or "guided meditation"), and the therapist uncovered some apparently repressed memories that indicate I was sexually abused as a child." Suppose, too, that although the client did not suspect abuse until it was diagnosed, his or her symptoms make the diagnosis a reasonable possibility. How can a therapist be true to the client's needs and open to the possibility that there was sexual abuse, without colluding in a convenient diagnosis that may exhibit more evidence of suggestion than therapeutic observation and fact? (Sheehan & McConkey, 1993; Yapko, 1993a, 1993b).

First and foremost, a therapist must not jump quickly to the conclusion that abuse occurred simply because it is plausible. Symptoms are not evidence for abuse. If the client has never mentioned being molested and has never previously identified himself or herself as an abuse survivor, the therapist should generally not be the one to suggest it. There are, of course, times when a therapist has good reason to suspect abuse and deems it necessary to mention the possibility to the client. If there is resistance, however, the therapist should not pathologize it by interpreting it as "denial," but should strive instead to create an atmosphere in which the client may eventually make the decision as to whether or not the issue should be pursued.

A therapist should never simply assume that a client who cannot remember much from childhood is repressing traumatic memories or is in denial. Believe it or not, there are individuals with a here-and-now or future-oriented quality to their subjective experiences whose recollections about childhood are quite impoverished because they do not think or care very much about remembering it. Furthermore, accepting the theory of traumatically based amnesia as an explanation for the lack of memories from infancy or earliest childhood flies in the face of developmental research about cognitive maturation. Research consistently shows that memory is marginal, at best, before the age of two; before that age, children apparently do not have the mental structures to form long-term coherent memories. While "body memory" is a convenient construct to maintain a belief in infant memory, it is hardly objective.

In any case, no therapist should ever, either directly or indirectly, suggest abuse outside of a specific therapeutic context—certainly not to a client who is on the phone making a first appointment. Nor should the therapist ask leading questions that imply either a desired or correct answer. For example, don't ask questions like. "When were you abused? How did he/she abuse you?" In the hypnotic context, such suggestive questions are based on what we call presuppositions—they presuppose that abuse did happen and all that needs to be determined is when and how. Presuppositions can be useful in therapy; asking a client, "How will you feel when you discover you can have the kind of relationship you want?" engenders expectations of positive change in therapy. Presuppositions about the reality of abuse, on the other hand, can help create the very pathology that the therapist is presumably treating.

A client is most vulnerable to suggestion and to the untoward influence of leading questions when therapy begins to delve into painful life situations from the past, particularly from childhood. At this point, the therapist is likely to ask, "How old were you? Where were you? What was going on? Was anyone around? What was said in the interaction between you and this person?" Such questions are necessary when they are asked to determine what the client has experienced, but therapists should be careful that they don't slide into more leading questions, like, "Did you feel uncomfortable with the interaction? Can you recall how you were made to feel afraid and ashamed?"

Even if, after being asked nonleading, neutral questions, the client does remember a formerly repressed memory of abuse, the therapist should be open to the possibility of other external sources of influence in the client's life. Has he or she, for example, read extensively in the incest recovery literature, been pressured by a sibling, or been very active in a survivor group?

When planning to conduct a session aimed at uncovering sensitive information, including repressed memories of abuse, the therapist should consider videotaping or audiotaping the session, and even transcribing the questions that were asked. This kind of self-monitoring enables the clinician to better determine whether or not he or she inadvertently suggested the possibility of abuse, thus provoking ficti- tious "memories" to emerge in a compliant or task-motivated client. Given the damage unsupported child abuse allegations can cause, therapists should perhaps infuse a bit of tolerance for ambiguity and what really happened into their practice, particularly when the client reports that repressed memories have suddenly surfaced in abuse recovery groups, for example, or after she read recovery literature. In such ambiguous cases, it is probably wise to seek out corroboration of the abuse by obtaining medical and school records from the client's child-hood, and interviewing family and friends about reported incidents—the more external evidence the better.

Therapists also should be cautious about suggesting that clients cut off communication with their families. Among the most destructive aspects of the abuse epidemic is the splintering of families in the wake of allegations made by a son or daughter. Family members are not necessarily lying or in denial if they reject the accusations. The possibil-ity shouldn't be dismissed out of hand that they are telling the truth, or experiencing heartfelt doubts and confusion themselves about what really happened. Certainly, doubt is inherent in the context, particularly for nonabusing family members. They *have* to wonder whether the abuse really happened or not; if it did, they can come to accept the truth only through open communication. Even if there has been abuse, it is irresponsible to frame predictable doubts and disbelief as toxic denial and precipitously insist that the client abandon his or her parents and siblings. Unnecessarily tearing the family apart for the sake of "healing" is a bit like curing the disease but killing the patient.

Finally, therapists should reconsider the "no pain, no gain" philoso-phy of treatment. Much of the pressure to recover memories, whatever the cost, derives from a common belief that every gory detail of abuse must be remembered and worked through before the client can begin to get better. This theory does not work for everyone, especially not for all abuse survivors. Relentlessly doing memory work for long periods of time can actually make some clients worse. It forces them to bring up more of what they already feel unable to handle. Approaches that emphasize resource building rather than memory work can fare better and should be considered in formulating a treatment plan for a particu-lar individual.

As therapists who are predisposed to like and believe our clients, to empathize with their pain, and to take their side, we may be too willing to let slide what our critical faculties say when it comes to the literal truth of what they are telling us. Because child abuse is so terrible, we do not want to be in the position of doubting people who may have suffered horribly because of it. At the same time, claims that false accusations are made cannot be dismissed simply because they go against the grain of our therapeutic inclinations, or because they are politically incorrect, particularly when the consequences of such alle-gations—true or false—are so dire.

As therapists we like to think of ourselves as the good guys. We may assume that some therapists are harmful, but we have a hard time imagining that we may inadvertently hurt clients. Nonetheless, if, in our goal to combat child abuse, we deny our own power to negatively influence clients and unintentionally create the very problem we intend to treat, we are betraying our mission. Nobody—not survivors of genuine abuse nor those who mistakenly believe they were abused, nor the families of either—is helped by therapists who abdicate their responsibility to think critically and who deny the need to make distinctions between truth and falsehood.

REFERENCES

Blume, E. (1990). *Secret survivors.* New York: Ballantine.

Bower, G. (1981). Mood and memory. *American Psychologist, 36,* 129–148.

Dywan, J. & Bowers, K. (1983). The use of hypnosis to enhance recall. *Science, 222,* 184–185.

Fredrickson, R. (1992). *Repressed memories.* New York: Fireside.

Ganaway, G. (1991, August). *Alternative hypotheses regarding satanic ritual abuse memories.* Paper presented at the 99th Annual Convention of the American Psychological Association, San Francisco.

Holmes, D. (1990). The evidence of repression: An examination of sixty years of research. In J. Singer (Ed.), *Repression and dissociation: Implications for personality, theory, psychopathology and health* (pp. 85–102). Chicago: University of Chicago Press.

Kihlstrom, J. & Evans, F. (1979). Memory retrieval processes during post-hypnotic amnesia. In J. Kihlstrom & F. Evans (Eds.), *Functional disorders of memory* (pp. 179–218). Hillsdale, NJ: Erlbaum.

Labelle, L., Laurence, J-R., Nadon, R., & Perry, C. (1990). Hypnotizability, preference for an imagic-cognitive style and memory creation in hypnosis. *Journal of Abnormal Psychology, 99,* 222–228.

Laurence, J-R., Nadon, R., Nogrady, H., & Perry, C. (1986) Duality, dissociation, and memory creation in highly hypnotizable subjects. *International Journal of Clinical and Experimental Hypnosis, 34,* 4, 295–310.

Laurence, J-R. & Perry, C. (1983). Hypnotically created memory among highly hypnotizable subjects. *Science, 222,* 523–524.

Loftus, E. (1980). *Memory.* Reading, MA: Addison-Wesley.

Loftus, E. (1993). The reality of repressed memories. *American Psychologist, 48,* 5, 518–537.

Loftus, E. & Hoffman, H. (1989). Misinformation and memory: The creation of new memories. *Journal of Experimental Psychology: General, 118,* 100–104.

Loftus, E. & Yapko, M. (1995). Psychotherapy and the recovery of repressed memories. In T. Ney (Ed.), *Handbook of allegations of child sexual abuse.* New York: Brunner/Mazel.

Lynn. S., Milano, M, Weeks, J. (1992). Pseudomemory and age regression: An exploratory study. *American Journal of Clinical Hypnosis, 35,* 2, 129–137.

Lynn, S., Weekes, J., & Milano, M. (1989). Reality vs. suggestion: Pseudomemory in hypnotizable and simulating subjects. *Journal of Abnormal Psychology, 98,* 137–144.

Orne, M.T. (1979). The use and misuse of hypnosis in court. *International Journal of Clinical and Experimental Hypnosis, 7,* 311–341.

Scheflin, A. & Shapiro, J. (1989). *Trance on trial.* New York: Guilford.

Sheehan, P. & Grigg, L. (1985). Hypnosis, memory and the acceptance of an implausible cognitive set. *British Journal of Clinical and Experimental Hypnosis, 3,* 5–12.

Sheehan, P. & McConkey, K. (1993). Forensic hypnosis: The application of ethical guidelines. In J. Rhue, S. Lynn & I. Kirsch (Eds.), *Handbook of clinical hypnosis* (pp. 719–738). Washington, DC: American Psychological Association.

Sheehan, P., Statham, D., & Jamieson, G. (1991). Pseudomemory effects over time in the hypnotic setting. *Journal of Abnormal Psychology, 100,* 39–44.

Watkins, J. (1989). Hypnotic hypermnesia and forensic hypnosis: A cross-examination. *American Journal of Clinical Hypnosis, 32,* 2, 71–83.

Yapko, M. (1990). *Trancework: An introduction to the practice of clinical hypnosis* (2nd ed.). New York: Brunner/Mazel.

Yapko, M. (1993a, September/October). The seductions of memory. *Family Therapy Networker, 17,* 5, 30–37.

Yapko, M. (1993b). Are we uncovering traumas or creating them?: Hypnosis, regression, and suggestions of abuse. In L. Vandercreek, S. Knapp, & T. Jackson (Eds.), *Innovations in clinical practice: A source book* (Vol. 12) (pp. 519–527). Sarasota, FL: Professional Resource Press.

Yapko, M. (1994a). Suggestibility and repressed memories of abuse: A survey of psychotherapists' beliefs. *American Journal of Clinical Hypnosis, 36,* 163–171.

Yapko, M. (1994b). *Suggestions of abuse: True and false memories of childhood sexual trauma.* New York: Simon & Schuster.

23

RESISTING RESISTANCE

The literature pertaining to clinical hypnosis has generally had quite a bit to say about the issue of client resistance. Overwhelmingly, resistance was considered to be a manifestation of the client's defenses for coping with sensitive intrapsychic conflicts. "Proper" treatment was a confrontive inquiry about the resistance, first acknowledging it, next attempting to uncover its origin and function, and then collaborating on its resolution. From this perspective, resistance was always considered the client's problem, serving as an intrapsychic coping device requiring analysis and interpretation. When it interfered with the progress of therapy, as it inevitably did, the client was blamed as the saboteur. Accusations and interpretations were thrust at the client, who obviously "really didn't want to change," or perhaps was "too resistant to succeed."

Resistance is, for all intents and purposes, a force that works against the aims of therapy. Resistance has long been recognized as an integral and unavoidable component of the therapeutic process, and virtually every therapeutic approach I am aware of has roughly equivalent recognitions of its existence. Only the rationale for its existence and techniques for its acknowledgement and treatment differ from approach to approach.

Defining resistance as a force that works against the aims of therapy does not place blame on either the clinician or client. Rather than view people coming in voluntarily (dealing with persons in treatment involuntarily clearly differs in some ways) for help as not really wanting help, it seems much more practical to view resistance as a communication from the client about his or her limitations in relating to the world (of which the clinician is a part). In other words, resistance isn't a fixed property of the client, but rather can be viewed as a communication indicating the limits of what the client can and cannot do. Rather than blame the client, the communication can be accepted as a valid indication of the person's experience of himself or herself.

Placing this general perspective in the context of doing hypnosis, resistance is not necessarily an indication of unconscious sabotage on the part of the client. It is frequently the case that the client is simply making a choice not to respond in the desired way to suggestions for any of a variety of other reasons, each of which has a common denominator: The suggestion simply does not fit with the person's experience, and, in fact, may even contradict it. Resistance may be viewed as an interpersonal statement that says that whatever therapeutic strategies and maneuvers are being performed are not acceptable at some level(s) to the client.

Resistance is a very real force, and can be tied to one or both of the two main areas of treatment: resistance to formal hypnosis, and/or resistance to therapeutic progress (Brown & Fromm, 1986; Erickson & Rossi, 1979; Grinder & Bandler, 1981; Yapko, 1984).

RESISTANCE TO HYPNOSIS

Origins of resistance to hypnosis can be numerous. One of the most common is the fear of what will happen during the hypnotic process. If the client is misinformed about the nature of the hypnotic experience, he or she may fear it.

Resistance to hypnosis may also arise because of past failures associated with hypnosis, either from personal experience or the experience of credible others. Resistance may also arise from negative feelings toward the clinician (thus highlighting the value of rapport). Resistance may also arise from contextual variables such as the immediate environment, the client's mood, health, and even the weather.

Most resistance to hypnosis, however, is attributable to the quality of the suggestions, specifically how well they match the client's experience. To impose arbitrary suggestions on clients that they experience something *you* want them to experience (like an arm levitation) that has little relationship to what they are experiencing or want to experience is a basis for choosing not to follow your suggestion (Erickson & Rossi, 1981; Fezler, 1986; Haley, 1973; Hilgard, 1991; Levitan & Jevne, 1986; Lynn & Rhue, 1991).

RESISTANCE TO THERAPEUTIC PROGRESS

Resistance to the aims of therapy has an extensive overlap with the dynamics of resistance to hypnosis.

Origins of the resistance to the aims of treatment can be numerous. Blocks may arise because of the client's intrapsychic conflicts, i.e., ambivalences, that have been described in detail in psychodynamic writings.

Resistance to therapeutic progress may also be attributed to the type of intervention employed if it involves strategies and maneuvers that are unacceptable to the client. Furthermore, if the clinician is working at a rate faster or slower than his or her client, resistance may surface. Resistance may also arise from negative feelings toward the clinician, or even from their opposite—idealized, romantic feelings that place a clinician on a pedestal he or she will almost inevitably fall from. Finally, contextual variables play a role as well, including such factors as environmental conditions, client disposition and health, and the like. It should be apparent that all the sensitivity that goes into effective hypnosis is just a part of the larger therapeutic picture, for all the same guidelines apply (Booth, 1988; deShazer, 1984; Watzlawick, 1978; Zeig, 1980).

RESPONDING TO RESISTANCE

How to deal with the communication deemed "resistant" is, of course, a function of how you conceptualize it. How resistance is defined and whose responsibility it is thought to be will determine whether you view resistance as a property of the client, a property of the clinician (for example, Bandler & Grinder [1979] have flatly stated that there is no such thing as resistance, there are only poor therapists), or an interactional outcome of the two.

Accepting the resistance as a valid communication from the client prevents having to ascribe blame to one or the other person in the relationship (Erickson, 1959, 1964, 1965).

The basic utilization formula of "accept and utilize" applies here. In practice, it takes the form of being able to skillfully accept the client's response as a valid one while developing a way to utilize the response in the service of further suggestions.

By accepting the client's response as a valid one, the response can be built upon. This redefines the resistance as cooperative behavior. If the clinician defines everything the client does as cooperative, where is the resistance? Finding a way to make the nonconforming behavior an asset to the person can change the feeling attached to it substantially.

Responding to a client's resistances in a way that is accepting and nonconfrontational requires a great deal of flexibility and respect for the integrity of the client. Flexibility refers to the ability to have a variety of ways to get a point across without having to beat the client over the head with it. Flexibility means being willing to go the extra distance to operate on the client's level, joining his or her reality instead of expecting or demanding that he or she come to yours. It also means not having so rigid a set of expectations and procedures that you would not allow for unique, individual responses (Dolan, 1985; Erickson & Rossi, 1979, 1981; Erickson, Rossi & Rossi, 1976; Gilligan, 1987; Hammond, 1990).

CONCLUSION

Resistance to change is a basic feature of humankind. We spend much of our lives trying to build a ritualized pattern of behavior so as to expend the least amount of physical and mental energy; after developing such a pattern, we complain of "being stuck in a rut."

Resistance doesn't always show up in detectable ways (some are so unconscious and subtle), and resistance can't always be used in the service of change. Some clients simply will not change, others only slightly. The discussion of resistance in this chapter is intended to present the idea that much of resistance is interpersonal, arising from a demanding, insensitive approach. Furthermore, other resistances relate to a lack of appreciation for the role of the symptom in the person's life. A greater number of interventions will succeed when the clinician is able to get a single point across in a large number of ways, using the feedback from each unique individual as his or her guide for knowing what to do as well as what not to.

REFERENCES

Bandler, R. & Grinder, J. (1979). *Frogs into princes*. Moab, UT: Real People Press.

Booth, P. (1988). Strategic therapy revisited. In J. Zeig & S. Lankton (Eds.), *Developing Ericksonian therapy: State of the art* (pp. 39–58). New York: Brunner/Mazel.

Brown, D. & Fromm, E. (1986). *Hypnotherapy and hypnoanalysis*. Hillsdale, NJ: Erlbaum.

deShazer, S. (1984). The death of resistance. *Family Process, 23*, 79–93.

Dolan, Y. (1985). *A path with a heart: Ericksonian utilization with resistant and chronic clients*. New York: Brunner/Mazel.

Erickson, M. (1959). Further clinical techniques of hypnosis: Utilization techniques. *American Journal of Clinical Hypnosis, 2*, 3–21.

Erickson, M. (1964). The burden of responsibility in effective psychotherapy. *American Journal of Clinical Hypnosis, 6*, 269–271.

Erickson, M. (1965). The use of symptoms as an integral part of hypnotherapy. *American Journal of Clinical Hypnosis, 8*, 57–65.

Erickson, M. & Rossi, E. (1979). *Hypnotherapy: An exploratory casebook*. New York: Irvington.

Erickson, M. & Rossi, E. (1981). *Experiencing hypnosis.* New York: Irvington.

Erickson, M., Rossi, E. & Rossi, S. (1976). *Hypnotic realities.* New York: Irvington.

Fezler, W. (1986). Clients who can't concentrate or who become more anxious during induction. In B. Zilbergeld, M. Edelstein & D. Araoz (Eds.), *Hypnosis: Questions and answers* (pp. 132–134). New York: Norton.

Gilligan, S. (1987). *Therapeutic trances: The cooperation principle in Ericksonian hypnotherapy.* New York: Brunner/Mazel.

Grinder, J. & Bandler, R. (1981). *Trance-formations: Neuro-Linguistic Programming and the structure of hypnosis.* Moab, UT: Real People Press.

Haley, J. (1973). *Uncommon therapy.* New York: Norton.

Hammond, D. (Ed.) (1990). *Handbook of hypnotic suggestions and metaphors.* New York: Norton.

Hilgard, E. (1991). A neodissociation interpretation of hypnosis. In S. Lynn & J. Rhue (Eds.), *Theories of hypnosis: Current models and perspectives* (pp. 83–104). New York: Guilford.

Johnson, L. (1988). Naturalistic techniques with the "difficult" patient. In J. Zeig & S. Lankton (Eds.), *Developing Ericksonian therapy: State of the art* (pp. 397–413). New York: Brunner/Mazel.

Levitan, A. & Jevne, R. (1986). Patients fearful of hypnosis. In B. Zilbergeld, M. Edelstein & D. Araoz (Eds.), *Hypnosis: Questions and answers* (pp. 81–86). New York: Norton.

Lynn, S. & Rhue, J. (1991). An integrative model of hypnosis: In S. Lynn & J. Rhue (Eds.), *Theories of hypnosis: Current models and perspectives* (pp. 397–438). New York: Guilford.

Watzlawick, P. (1978). *The language of change.* New York: Basic Books.

Yapko, M. (1984). The implications of the Ericksonian and Neuro-Linguistic Programming approaches for responsibility of therapeutic outcomes. *American Journal of Clinical Hypnosis, 27,* 137–143.

Zeig, J. (Ed.) (1980). *A teaching seminar with Milton H. Erickson, M.D.* New York: Brunner/Mazel.

24

HYPNOTIC HAZARDS AND ETHICAL GUIDELINES

In the earlier chapter addressing misconceptions about hypnosis, one of the misconceptions discussed briefly concerned the potential harm to a client undergoing treatment through hypnosis. In that discussion, I made the point that hypnosis is a tool, not a therapy, and that it could be applied skillfully or it could be misused and potentially harm the client. This places full responsibility on the clinician to exercise caution and sensitivity in the use of hypnotic techniques.

By dealing more directly with the client's unconscious mind and intrapsychic dynamics, the clinician has the opportunity to gain access to an internal world that is delicately balanced. To be insensitive to the powerful emotions that may be triggered, traditionally called an "abreaction," can place the client in jeopardy emotionally, not to mention wasting an opportunity to do some real healing. If a clinician is uncomfortable in dealing with strong emotional associations that may be triggered by what was originally intended to be the most soothing of hypnotic experiences, the choice exists to either *get* comfortable or avoid doing any work of real emotional impact (thus doing therapy in an entirely intellectual style).

In this chapter I would like to discuss some of the potential unexpected reactions to hypnosis that necessitate a healthy respect for the power of the tool.

Before you begin to fantasize unspeakably horrible possibilities, let me assure you of a couple of things. First, if you are respectful of the innate integrity of your client, you will avoid virtually all of the potential pitfalls. Second, if you can appreciate that abreactions have great potential therapeutic value through the release of insight and emotion if guided skillfully, they won't have to be feared. That doesn't mean they have to be encouraged either, but they can be viewed as an open door to a powerful therapeutic experience.

There are no dangers attributable to the hypnotic state in and of itself. Whatever difficulties may arise as a result of hypnotic experiences have to do with the associations triggered by all the communication elements present in the interaction. These include the relationship between clinician and client, the communication style employed, the specific suggestion content, the contextual variables, and, most importantly, the client's intrapersonal communications (Frauman, Lynn & Brentar, 1993; Judd, Burrows & Dennerstein, 1985; MacHovec, 1986).

Problems may arise in the indiscriminate use of hypnosis because of some of the very reasons I will describe now in identifying potential difficulties and their resolution.

SYMPTOM SUBSTITUTION

One of the most common arguments against the use of hypnosis concerns the potential for "symptom substitution." Symptom substitution refers to the onset of a new symptom, perhaps but not necessarily a worse one, in the place of the old symptom removed during treatment. In order for one to charge hypnosis with this potential liability, hypnosis must be viewed as a symptomatic treatment as opposed to a more dynamic approach addressing underlying root causes. The dynamic theory is that there is a psychic energy associated with internal conflicts that is relieved by the development of a symptom—an outlet for the energy. By removing the outlet, the energy must be redirected elsewhere and a new outlet developed. Other "symptomatic" approaches, most notably behaviorism, have faced this same charge.

In the case of hypnosis, there is a twist that makes the response to the criticism somewhat complex. Hypnosis *can* be used symptomatically (standardization of approach is an example), and, in my opinion, is used this way all too often, partially because of the lack of laws regulating formal training and the competent practice of hypnosis. Simple, direct suggestion aimed at a target symptom can be used by untrained laypersons with no real understanding of the issues presented throughout this chapter in particular and this book in general. Without an understanding of the role of symptom in a person's life and the related dynamics, symptom substitution can be (but isn't necessarily) an unwanted, unexpected outcome.

The twist is that while hypnosis can be used symptomatically, its greatest strength is derived from its ability to be used in a more substantive way, such as in addressing a symptom's underlying dynamics and consequences. It is this type of practice I wanted to promote throughout this book through my consideration of so many issues and concepts associated with the responsible practice of clinical hypnosis (Rosen, 1960; Spiegel & Spiegel, 1987; Weitzenhoffer, 1989).

FAILURE TO REMOVE SUGGESTIONS

A common fear expressed to me by my students concerns the failure to remove suggestions. With all the things there are to occupy the clinician's mind in doing hypnosis (formulating meaningful suggestions while closely observing and utilizing client responses), what happens if the clinician forgets to remove a suggestion?

The response to this seemingly hazardous condition is a relatively simple one. The suggestions for particular responses of the person in hypnosis are state-specific. In other words, they are operative only as long as the person is in the hypnotic state. There is no carryover of the hypnotically obtained responses into the client's "waking" state unless there has been a suggestion to do so. You may remember that that is the main purpose of the posthypnotic suggestion—to allow the responses obtained in hypnosis to generalize to other contexts. Without the posthypnotic suggestions (either from the client to himself or herself or from the clinician) to carry the response over to some other context, the response is just an interesting one observable during hypnosis. Thus, if the clinician forgets to remove suggestions given during hypnosis at the end of the hypnotic process, the suggestion is highly likely to dissipate automatically upon disengagement. If the exception occurs and the client continues to experience a suggestion that was not intended posthypnotically, it is likely that the client has somehow given himself or herself the posthypnotic suggestion to do so. Hypnosis may be reintroduced and the suggestion removed if desired (Brentar, Lynn, Carlson & Kurzhals, 1992; Kleinhauz & Beran, 1984; Orne, 1965; Weitzenhoffer, 1989).

SPONTANEOUS REGRESSION AND ABREACTION

The terms "spontaneous regression" and "abreaction" are not synonymous terms, but rather are so closely related in their association that I have chosen to discuss them together in this section. A spontaneous regression is the experience of repressed past experiences coming into awareness. Abreaction has been defined earlier in this chapter as the expression of pent-up emotions. Together, these two account for the often unexpected emotionalism that makes hypnosis such a powerful tool. When you are doing something seemingly as simple as a general relaxation procedure, a client may flash on some word or image that you use that is associated to an emotionally charged memory, bringing up feelings of intense hurt, pain, anger, or the like.

The spontaneous regression back to some unpleasant memory is an indicator of what is commonly called "unfinished business," experiences requiring further resolution. Sometimes the repression is so great that the material remains out of consciousness even during hypnosis, and the person complains of a headache or some other such discomfort after the hypnotic experience.

Even the most skilled clinician cannot know what land mines are in the client's unconscious waiting to be tripped during therapy or hypnosis. Each human being has his or her own unique personal history and idiosyncratic associations to words and experiences. What seems like a neutral term to one person may be the trigger to some intense personal experience to another. Therefore, the possibility of doing hypnosis without ever producing an abreaction is highly unlikely. Some clinicians, on the other hand, instigate abreactions by a sort of "psychological voyeurism," assuming that intense emotionality is therapeutically necessary as well as fascinating to observe.

Abreactions can manifest themselves in a variety of ways, including crying, hyperventilation, trembling of the body (or specific body parts), hysterical conversions, premature disengagement from hypnosis, hallucinations, delusions, and autistic-like rocking motions. These behaviors are not automatically indicative of an abreaction, but they should be responded to cautiously and sensitively. The first and foremost thing to remember is this: *You can feel comfortable asking your client to describe his or her experience.* Give protective suggestions and be supportive of his or her experiences, using the general "accept and utilize" formula. The person has opened up with some sensitive information, and it is a waste to let the moment pass and do nothing. Allow the abreaction, but be helpful to the client in helping him or her reach a new perspective on the experience. After all, that's what therapy is for, isn't it? You can't change the past, only attitudes toward it.

Use calming suggestions, and even if the reaction is wholly unexpected you know now to expect the unexpected. Make sure your voice is soothing and confident. In general, the best thing you can do is use hypnosis to resolve the situation and attain some closure. Even if your client's hour is up, your responsibility to that person isn't over. Make certain he or she can leave in a collected manner.

If a client opens up with some sensitive information that you are simply not equipped to handle for whatever reason, I suggest that you make sure the client is immediately referred to an appropriate helping professional (thus the value of a good referral list) (Crasilneck & Hall, 1985; Feldman, 1985; Hammond, 1990; Kroger, 1977; Spiegel & Spiegel, 1987; Spiegel, 1993; Yapko, 1992).

ETHICAL GUIDELINES

The above descriptions of potential difficulties that may arise in the use of hypnosis indirectly comment on the need for formal education in the dynamics of human behavior, the need to be respectful of the integrity of each human being, and the need to know your own limits in providing therapeutic interventions.

As a helping professional, you are assumed to have only the best of intentions for your clients. It is also asssumed that you will use the understandings of human nature and the capacity for interpersonal influence you have in a constructive way. Therefore, there is only a superficial coverage of ethical guidelines provided below:

1. The number one priority is to help, not hurt. If you feel that, for *any* reason, you are unable to work well with either the person or the problem presented to you, then evaluate honestly whether it would be best to refer that client elsewhere—and do so when appropriate.

2. A professional's responsibility is to educate, not show off. Hypnosis lends itself to both, and it is my sincere hope that the hypnotic phenomena you are learning to induce are used and/or demonstrated only in appropriate clinical or educational settings.

3. Have your relationship with your client(s) as clearly defined as possible, including the nature of the intervention, the duration, the cost, the expectations, evaluation points, etc. Involving and educating your client will most certainly make for a better, more productive relationship.

4. Do not go beyond your range of expertise, or misrepresent yourself. Human problems are very complex and can't be reduced to a paragraph of dynamics. If you feel you are out of your depth when presented with a problem, refer the person to someone better able to meet his or her needs.

5. Presenting misinformation and/or the use of indirect techniques will sometimes be judged to be the best approach. Be careful—such approaches can help a client, but they can also backfire. Have alternatives prepared every step of the way by thinking your intervention strategy through. In other words, be prepared!

6.   Always involve, when appropriate, the proper qualified health professionals. For example, when working on organically based symptoms, unless you are a physician, you should have a medical referral and medical clearance to work with the problem. Practicing medicine (psychology, nutrition, etc.) without a license or without adequate knowledge and backup is nothing short of irresponsible.

More importantly, I repeat my warning to never go beyond your range of expertise. Using hypnotic techniques without adequate knowledge is potentially dangerous, and damaging someone through ignorance is unforgivable (Frauman, Lynn & Brentar, 1993; Gravitz, Mallet, Munyon & Gerton, 1982; Sheehan & McConkey, 1993; Steere, 1984; Wall, 1991; Zeig, 1985).

CONCLUSION

The concepts and techniques presented in this chapter are ones that rank as some of the most important in this book. It is my hope that this chapter helps sensitizing you to the issues associated with the responsible practice of hypnosis.

Hypnosis as a tool is of potentially great value, and its use can grow at a faster rate in the professional community when each practitioner who uses hypnosis does so in a sensitive way.

REFERENCES

Brentar, J., Lynn, S., Carlson, B. & Kurzhals, R. (1992). Controlled research on hypnotic aftereffects: The post-hypnotic experience questionnaire. In W. Bongartz (Ed.), *Hypnosis: 175 years after Mesmer* (pp. 179–201). Konstanz, Germany: University of Konstanz Press.

Crasilneck, H. & Hall, J. (1985). *Clinical hypnosis: Principles and applications.* Orlando: Grune & Stratton.

Feldman,S. (1985). Abreaction revisited: A strategic and interpersonal perspective. In J. Zeig (Ed.), *Ericksonian psychotherapy: Vol. 1, Structures* (pp. 338–358). New York: Brunner/Mazel.

Frauman, D., Lynn, S. & Brentar, J. (1993). Prevention and therapeutic management of "negative effects" in hypnotherapy. In J. Rhue, S. Lynn & I. Kirsch (Eds.), *Handbook of clinical hypnosis* (pp. 95–120). Washington, DC: American Psychological Association.

Gravitz, M., Mallet, J., Munyon. P. & Gerton, M. (1982). Ethical considerations in the professional applications of hypnosis. In M. Rosenbaum (Ed.), *Ethics and values in psychotherapy: A guidebook.* New York: Free Press.

Hammond, D. (Ed.) (1990). *Handbook of suggestions and metaphors.* New York: Norton.

Judd, F., Burrows, G. & Dennerstein, L. (1985). The dangers of hypnosis: A review. *Australian Journal of Clinical and Experimental Hypnosis, 13*, 1–15.

Kleinhauz, M. & Beran, B. (1984). Misuse of hypnosis: A factor in psychopathology. *American Journal of Clinical Hypnosis, 26*, 283–290.

Kroger, W. (1977). *Clinical and experimental hypnosis* (2nd ed.). Philadelphia: Lippincott.

MacHovec, F. (1986). *Hypnosis complications: Prevention and risk management.* Springfield, IL: C.C. Thomas.

Orne, M. (1965). Undesirable effects of hypnosis: The determinants and management. *International Journal of Clinical and Experimental Hypnosis, 13*, 226–237.

Rosen, H. (1960). Hypnosis: Applications and misapplications. *Journal of the American Medical Association, 17*, 5, 976–979.

Sheehan, P. & McConkey, K. (1993). Forensic hypnosis: The application of ethical guidelines. In J. Rhue, S. Lynn & I. Kirsch (Eds.), *Handbook of clinical hypnosis* (pp. 719–738). Washington, DC: American Psychological Association.

Spiegel, D. (1993). Hypnosis in the treatment of post-traumatic stress disorders. In J. Rhue, S. Lynn & I. Kirsch (Eds.), *Handbook of clinical hypnosis* (pp. 493–508). Washington, DC: American Psychological Association.

Spiegel, H. & Spiegel, D. (1987). *Trance and treatment: Clinical uses of hypnosis.* Washington, DC: American Psychiatric Press.

Steere, J. (1984). *Ethics in clinical psychology.* London: Oxford University Press.

Wall, T. (1991). Ethics—The royal road to legitimacy. *American Journal of Clinical Hypnosis, 34*, 73–78.

Weitzenhoffer, A. (1989). *The practice of hypnotism* (Vol. 2). New York: John Wiley & Sons.

Yapko, M. (1992). *Hypnosis and the treatment of depressions.* New York: Brunner/Mazel.

Zeig, J. (1985). Ethical issues in hypnosis: Informed consent and training standards. In J. Zeig (Ed.), *Ericksonian psychotherapy: Vol. 1, Structures* (pp. 459–473). New York: Brunner/Mazel.

25

GOING DEEPER INTO HYPNOSIS

I don't know who it was that originally made the observation, "The more you know, the more you know how little you know." Whoever it was, I wonder if he or she was talking about hypnosis when making that comment. Well, probably not. But it holds true for the study of hypnosis nonetheless. I hope that by the time you have reached this concluding chapter, you will have discovered the richness and complexity that hypnosis as a communication tool affords.

One of the most frustrating things to professionals in the field of clinical hypnosis is the fact that people with far less education in hypnosis than this introductory level book provides are engaged in providing services to the public that they are not qualified to provide. A second source of frustration to those in the field of clinical hypnosis lies in the observation that many people take courses in hypnosis and then, when the course is over, don't utilize the acquired skills, which soon fade into the past. My belief is that when the practice of hypnosis was limited to the ritualistic and time-consuming techniques of the past, hypnosis as a tool was limited in its effectiveness and applicability. I further believe that as hypnosis is broadened from "hocus-pocus" to a model of deliberate and effective communication, increasing numbers of professionals can integrate hypnotic patterns into their work. My goal was not and is not to transform readers of this book into "official hypnotists." Rather, my goal has been to provide you with an introduction to a field that is dynamic, evolving, and a source of valuable insight about people and therapy. Even if you never formally induce hypnosis in the remainder of your life, my guess is that you'll reflexively think twice before saying something like, "Don't think about what's bothering you." From this introduction to the field, I hope that you will be sufficiently íntrigued by the range of possibilities hypnosis as a tool has to offer that you will be encouraged to continue developing your skills with it. There are many ways to do so.

There are numerous books and publications that deal with the subject of clinical hypnosis. The many references contained in this book are just the tip of the iceberg, but they can provide a starting point for meaningful reading. The bibliographies in journals dedicated to the field of hypnosis are invaluable sources from which to acquire the most recent concepts and approaches in the professional practice of hypnosis. Two major hypnosis organizations publish scientific journals. The information on where to write in order to attain membership in these organizations and in order to subscribe to their journals is listed below:

The American Journal of Clinical Hypnosis
published by the American Society of Clinical Hypnosis
For membership (includes journal) write to:
2200 East Devon Avenue
Suite 291
Des Plaines, Illinois 60018
Tel.: (708) 297-3317; FAX: (708) 297-7309
address subscriptions to "Business Manager"

The International Journal of Clinical and Experimental Hypnosis
published by
The Society for Clinical and Experimental Hypnosis, Inc.
For membership (includes journal) write to:
The Society for Clinical and Experimental Hypnosis, Inc.
128-A Kings Park Drive
Liverpool, New York 13090
Tel. & FAX: (315) 652-7299

While the importance of reading current literature cannot be overstated, neither can the value of further experiential training. Beyond the training many universities now provide and the private training programs offered by many professionals, the hypnosis organizations listed above provide excellent training programs to qualified professionals both on national and local levels. The American Society of Clinical Hypnosis (ASCH) has branches in major cities, with training programs held routinely. They also provide a certification that assures consumers of your extensive training.

The Milton H. Erickson Foundation in Phoenix, Arizona, is dedicated to the advancement of Ericksonian hypnosis, and presents national and international Erickson Congresses—major meetings at which scholarly papers, demonstrations, workshops, and discussions are held over several days solely on the topic of clinical hypnosis. In addition to sponsoring the Congresses, the Foundation publishes an interesting newsletter three times per year that includes a guide to when and where training programs will be offered. To get on the Foundations's mailing list, write or call them at the following address:

> The Milton H. Erickson Foundation, Inc.
> 3606 North 24th Street
> Phoenix, Arizona 85016
> Tel. (602) 956-6196; FAX: (602) 956-0519

In addition to the organizations mentioned above, there are smaller, often more specialized groups that are too numerous to mention here. The quality of training, the eligibility for membership, and the goals and functions of the various groups differ greatly. Affiliation with an organization should ultimately be a synergistic relationship, not a one-sided one, and selectivity is therefore encouraged.

At the close, it is difficult for me to assess whether or not I have been able to transmit my respect and appreciation for hypnosis effectively. I frequently found myself wanting to say much, much more about each of the topics presented, but felt obligated to preserve this text's integrity as a concise introduction to the field. There is much more to be said about the human mind, personality, communication, and hypnosis. Our current understandings are ever-expanding, and there appears to be no upper limit as to how much can eventually be known. I hope you will find many ways to make good use of all that hypnosis makes possible.

Name Index

Adrian, C., 114
Alman, B., 19, 34, 65, 69, 119, 138, 139
Araoz, D., 8, 16, 17, 35, 128, 139
Aronson, E., 40
Atkinson, G., 54

Bandler, R., 15, 27, 62, 64, 65, 74, 76, 77, 78, 79, 84, 88, 92, 97, 102, 103, 104, 116, 117, 131, 135, 161, 162
Banks, W., 33
Banyai, E., 20, 50
Barabasz, A., 135
Barber, J., 16, 31, 39, 52, 114
Barber, T., 8, 53
Barker, P., 79, 103, 132
Bart, C., 53
Bates, S., 40, 91
Beahrs, J., 65
Bemis, C., 31
Benjamin, H., 137
Benson, H., 60
Bentell, R., 117
Beran, B., 167
Bertrand, L., 42, 53
Bliss, S., 136
Bloom, P., 115
Blume, E., 152
Booth, P., 86, 162
Bordeaux, J., 54
Bower, G., 153
Bowers, K., 24, 153
Braun, B., 136
Brentar, J., 18, 40, 86, 166, 167, 170

Brown, D., 31, 35, 45, 46, 72, 103, 113, 132, 135, 137, 161
Brunet, A., 45
Burrows, G., 136, 166

Cardena, E., 115
Carlin, A., 65
Carlson, B., 167
Carney, R., 65
Carol, M., 60
Chavez, J., 8, 31, 113, 137
Cheek, D., 33, 45, 118, 130, 137
Chopra, D., 137
Cialdini, R., 38
Coe, W., 25, 39, 40, 95, 97, 117
Cohen, S., 31, 92
Cooper, L., 111, 118
Council, J., 12, 20, 42, 59
Crasilneck, H., 35, 71, 113, 139, 169
Crawford, H., 45, 57, 135
Crowley, R., 103, 132

Davidson, T., 24
Davis, L., 53
Dennerstein, L., 166
de Shazer, S., 111, 162
Detrick, D., 51
Dewey, M., 117
Diamond, M., 17, 39
Dixon, M., 45
Dolan, Y., 163
Dywan, J., 153

Edelstein, M., 108
Edgette, Ja., 107

175

Subject Index

About the Author

MICHAEL D. YAPKO, Ph.D., is author of the bestselling *Suggestions of Abuse: True and False Memories of Childhood Sexual Trauma.* He is a clinical psychologist in private practice in Solana Beach, California and is Director of the Milton H. Erickson Institute of San Diego. He is also the author and editor of numerous books, including *Trancework: An Introduction to the Practice of Clinical Hypnosis.* He is a well-known speaker both nationally and internationally and is an influential authority on such topics as depression, Ericksonian psychotherapy, and sexual trauma.

Also by
Michael D. Yapko

SUGGESTIONS OF ABUSE: TRUE AND FALSE MEMORIES
OF CHILDHOOD SEXUAL TRAUMA

HYPNOSIS AND THE TREATMENT OF DEPRESSIONS:
STRATEGIES FOR CHANGE

USING HYPNOSIS IN TREATING DEPRESSION
(4-CASSETTE AUDIOTAPE PROGRAM)

TRANCEWORK: AN INTRODUCTION TO THE PRACTICE OF
CLINICAL HYPNOSIS

THE CASE OF VICKI: PATTERNS OF TRANCEWORK
(VIDEOTAPE)

BRIEF THERAPY APPROACHES TO TREATING ANXIETY
AND DEPRESSION
(EDITOR)

WHEN LIVING HURTS: DIRECTIVES FOR TREATING
DEPRESSION